THE LEADERSHIP LIBRARY

V O L U M E   2

LIBERATING THE LEADER'S PRAYER LIFE

Other books in The Leadership Library

Well-Intentioned Dragons by Marshall Shelley

THE LEADERSHIP LIBRARY

Volume

2

Liberating the Leader's Prayer Life

Terry Muck

Carol Stream, Illinois

WORD BOOKS
PUBLISHER
WACO, TEXAS
A DIVISION OF
WORD, INCORPORATED

LIBERATING THE LEADER'S PRAYER LIFE

Copyright © 1985 by Christianity Today, Inc.

A LEADERSHIP/Word Book. Copublished by Christianity Today, Inc. and Word, Inc. Distributed by Word Books.

Designed by Tim Botts

Cover art by Joe Van Severen

Unless otherwise marked, all Scripture quotations are from the New International Version of the Bible, copyright 1978 by the New York International Bible Society.

Library of Congress Cataloging in Publication Data

Muck, Terry
Liberating the Leader's Prayer Life

(The Leadership Library; volume 2)
1. Prayer. I. Title. II. Series
BV210.2.M79 1985   248.3'2   85-5766
ISBN 0-917463-05-6

Printed in the United States of America

To my colleagues
at Christianity Today, Inc.
With them I have learned
the joys of combining
leadership and prayer.
They are my best models.

C O N T E N T S

PREFACE

P. T. Forsyth, in *The Soul of Prayer*, said, "It is a formidable thing to write on prayer. Perhaps no one ought to undertake it unless he has spent more toil in the practice of prayer than on its principles."[1] I don't qualify as one who has spent more toil on practice than theory. So when research by LEADERSHIP Journal indicated our readers felt a need for a book on the Christian leader's prayer life, I had two options: not write the book myself or get help doing it.

Because I was personally intrigued by the subject and wanted to do the book, we chose the second option: Get help. And get it from the people most interested—Christian leaders themselves. Few of them would claim to be proficient prayer practitioners either. But if scores of us could pool our experiences with prayer, we might learn something about how God and human beings communicate.

I quickly learned Christian leaders love prayer; I also found they carry a certain amount of guilt about not praying enough or not doing it well. Yet they want to work at it. After dozens of interviews with church leaders about the practical steps they have taken to improve their attitudes and practice, two resources were mentioned most:

The Bible. Leaders mentioned not only the familiar passages on prayer but the biblical prayer giants who serve as models. What drove godly leaders in Scripture to their knees? Famine? Goliath? Crucifixion? We then discussed what the famines, goliaths, and crucifixions are that we face today. What made it hard for Moses to be obedient, loving, thankful, and contrite? We considered what that means for Christian leaders today.

Others in ministry. I also learned that church leaders want to hear from their peers—men and women who are fighting the same battles. Of course, church leaders recognize the uniqueness of each person's prayer life. One said, "I know that others can't do my praying for me. And it's unlikely their methods will work perfectly for me. But perhaps I can find something transferable." We have included prayer experiences of others in the hope that you'll find something of practical value.

Those interviewed were ordinary church leaders. No Praying Hydes or David Brainerds who spent eight hours a day on their prayer carpets. We didn't try to isolate spectacular success stories, although almost to a person, these church leaders had wonderful stories of answered prayer ready to be told. Interviewees were barely screened in any way. If they would agree to an interview, we talked to them about prayer.

The results were uplifting. We live in an insane world, a world that hungers for God. And the way to God is through prayer. Billy Graham has called the eighties the decade of prayer. George Gallup tells us that 86 percent of those in the United States, both churched and unchurched, say they pray to God.[2] Christian leaders are caught up in that hunger, and it has created extraordinary interest in personal devotion.

The language of this book is "this worldly." At times the sentences and paragraphs reflect the disciplines of psychology, philosophy, sociology, and other sciences. But the spirit of the book comes from an entirely different, "other-worldly" source. It resides in the intimate relationship between God and his creation, mankind. Indeed, it is the love of God that must bleed through on every page, or the book will fail. Because we are human, we must use the earthly, the mundane to proclaim the eternal—but let us never forget that only when seen by the light of God's love does the mundane make any sense at all.

O N E

TO LEAD OR TO PRAY?

Be not forgetful of prayer. Every time you pray, if your prayer is sincere there will be new feeling and new meaning in it, which will give you fresh courage, and you will understand that prayer is an education.

FYODOR DOSTOEVSKI

What frustrates Christian leaders about prayer? Perhaps it has something to do with the differences between leading and praying. When a random sample of people was asked what the term *leadership* brought to mind, they responded with words like authority, decisiveness, confidence, and power. The word *prayer*, on the other hand, evoked words such as humility, pleading, and powerlessness.

The difference illustrates a conflict Christian leaders face. As leaders, they preach, counsel, and organize with efficiency. Leaders must see that things get done. They plan, decide, act, and evaluate. In most people's minds, leadership means the ability to solve problems.

This expectation extends beyond administrative duties. Sometimes it seems Christian leaders are expected to have answers to most of life's problems. Even the leader's personal spirituality is held up as a public example of a faith that works. The writer to the Hebrews called it a "faith we should imitate" (13:7).

Men and women of prayer, however, operate in a different sphere, where feelings of inadequacy and helplessness must predominate. Those feelings sometimes conflict with the tasks of ministry. Jeff Ginn, pastor of Noelridge Baptist Church in Cedar Rapids, Iowa, notes: "We all want our ministries to have results. We see our work schedule as a time for production. If I have to choose between my quiet time and a meeting with a young Christian, often I'll choose the young Christian because that meeting will produce something tangible in my ministry.

"The results of prayer aren't quite so tangible. The need for prayer pulls at me over the long haul, but it's not an urgent pull. A fish on the line is an urgent pull. Getting the boat in the right place with the right fishing tackle all oiled and ready to go is a far less urgent task, yet it can make the difference in whether the fish is landed."

Prayer does prepare us for the more tangible ministry tasks. It makes us better leaders. But the effects of prayer can't be measured in terms of problems solved per square inch. For the administrator, decisiveness that averts a $5,000 mistake by the building contractor is laudatory. In the prayer closet, the same quick decision making may be counterproductive—it might lead to the oversight of an important spiritual subtlety only quietness and patience can discern. Or, willingness to take responsibility for a hair-splitting ethical decision concerning Mrs. Smith's wayward son is a sign of strong leadership. Someone must do it. But in the prayer closet, that same willingness to make firm decisions in ambiguous circumstances may blunt a creative paradox God could use to teach spiritual truth. Administrative problems follow the rules of cause and effect; prayer operates by God's unpublished rules.

When cause and effect meet divine guidance, they often clash. The result? The roles of confident decision maker and humble penitent do regular battle in the soul of the Christian leader, and an incomplete, guilt-ridden prayer life may plague the ministry.

"My spiritual pilgrimage is like the front and back yards of my life," says C. D. Monismith, a pastor in Salem, Oregon. "The front yard is for public view—manicured, watered, weed free, and beautiful. The back yard is not so good. It's utilitarian; it's mowed but not manicured. Some weeds grow around the edges, and there are patches of brown. It could use watering. My front yard is like my corporate, public spiritual life. My back yard is like my personal prayer life. I'd like to know how other pastors manicure the back yard as well as the front."

Monismith speaks for many of his peers. Most Christian leaders desire a stronger prayer life. In a survey of LEADERSHIP readers (80 percent of whom are pastors or pastoral staff) done two years ago, 56 percent of the respondents expressed dissatisfaction with the amount of time they spent in prayer. Yet when asked how much time they did spend in prayer, over 50 percent said they prayed more than twenty minutes a day, almost three times the seven daily minutes other surveys indicate is average for the general Christian population.

Further, Christian leaders like to read and learn about prayer. Articles on the subject published in Christian magazines get high readership. When asked, *What is the single area of leadership you'd most like help with?* Christian leaders most often responded, "My own spiritual walk with God."[1] For this group of people, where prayer is concerned, more is better.

But "more" is not easy to come by. Our thirst for prayer is camouflaged by our hunger for less nutritious food. The attractions of a nonpraying life—busyness that fills up the hours, distractions that divert attention, temptations that distort priorities—block our efforts to increase praying time.

Many of these blocks are not unique to the Christian leader. Laziness, impatience, rebelliousness, and unconfessed sin plague everyone. Lifestyles that include jam-packed schedules, jangling telephones, raucous radios, and fast-paced television programs don't offer quiet opportunities for reflection. Modern society is characterized by thinkers who put prayer in the same category as witch hazel and other old wives' tales. Immanuel Kant called prayer "a superstitious vanity"; Sigmund Freud said it was a way of "shuffling off one's human responsibilities"; Ludwig Feuerbach said it resulted in "religious alienation." It's no wonder prayer sometimes seems under attack.[2]

Three Blocks to Prayer

In addition to the common pressures, Christian leaders face three that are unique to their vocation. One is the expectation placed on them by historical roles. Modern church leaders still labor under clerical traditions traced back to the fourth-century monastic movement when clerics began to be viewed as professionals separated from the laity. Monks established specific hours of prayer—seven or eight times a day set aside for on-the-knees devotion. Had this remained a monastic practice, all would have been fine. But soon it became generalized for all clergy, whether withdrawn from the world or not. The Emperor Justinian, sounding a little like a contemporary bishop, berated the overworked parish priests for "neglecting a task [prayer] to which you are obliged by profession." The seven or eight *times* of daily prayer soon became seven or eight full *hours* of prayer a day—for monks especially, but sometimes for parish clergy too.[3]

Thereafter in the history of the church, whenever clergy reform became necessary, it was accompanied by a call for increased participation in prayer. There was nothing wrong with that in itself. We need frequently to be called back to our knees to pray. Unfortunately, the *form* suggested was usually realistic only for the full-time religious. For example, the Council of Reform in 817 recommended full participation by all clerics in the seven Hours of the Office, which by that time usually included full recitation of all 150 Psalms three times a day in addition to other prayers.

Even though the pressure of this was mitigated somewhat by church leaders like Benedict, who recognized the spiritual significance of work as well as prayer, the trend it set for clergy expectations remained. The heritage today can be seen in the question often asked the pastor, "But what else do you have to do all day besides prayer and study?" Usually this criticism is unthinking rather than vindictive. Most laymen, if questioned, would recognize the heavy administrative responsibilities of modern church leadership. Most would agree this makes spiritual work difficult. But subconsciously, the expectations remain. And it loads our Christian leaders with intense guilt about their prayer life.

Guilt also comes from the expectations of church leaders themselves. Many assume leadership roles in answer to God's call. Too often, though, the call is interpreted as a responsibility to personally fulfill the entire Great Commission. The faulty logic runs like this: "Saving the world required a perfect sacrifice: Christ. Since I'm not perfect, I must work even harder to save the world."

One pastor said: "The greatest relief of my young ministry was when I finally realized God could get his work done without me. That freed me to do even more for the Kingdom without loading myself with guilt for what I couldn't do." One's personal prayer life can suffer horribly from a self-induced messiah complex—or even an honest workaholic ethic fueled by popular maxims like "Wear out, don't rust out for Christ."

A third source of guilt is the natural bent of most church leaders toward rational methods of learning. Analytic thinking works for most areas of Bible study and theology. But the experience of prayer extends beyond the rational. Listen to people who want to talk about prayer. They start enthusiastically, but the words don't last long. The enthusiasts soon discover prayer is too central, too much a part of the core to be reduced to a series of convincing syllogisms. So they end up talking around it. They talk about great answers to prayer and their troubles in being consistent in prayer. But the experience itself eludes attempts to verbalize.

Prayer *is* a very private experience. One pastor whom several people suggested as a model of powerful praying noted that studies of other people's prayer lives run the risk of invasion of privacy: "There are areas of Christian experience, like marriage, that are almost too sacred for research. The 'how-to-do-it' books on prayer can show us the direction to the secret place and help us find time for the closed door, but who is the person who will attempt to define, delineate, and demonstrate what takes place there?"

For the rational, straight-thinking church leader, this can be a frustration. Why can't prayer be attacked like any one of a dozen problems solved this past year? We repaved the parking lot, helped Al Aronson work through his depression, and I planned my speaking engagements for the next year and penciled in preparation time for them all. But prayer . . .

In spite of these apparent contradictions, leadership responsibility and prayer are not incompatible. Many Christian leaders have successfully wedded the two and enjoy the marriage. The offspring is a fruitful ministry.

But the marriage works only when leadership and prayer are seen as a private partnership instead of jealous brothers competing for God's time. The conditions of the partnership are not difficult. In fact, they are really rather ordinary. The key is to match God's terms with the ordinaries of life.

TWO

THE EXTRAORDINARY IN THE ORDINARY

Ordinary people have an exciting time, while odd people are always complaining of the dullness of life. This is why the new novel dies so quickly and the old fairy tales endure forever. The old fairy tale makes the hero a normal, human boy. It is his adventures that are startling. They startle him because he is normal. But in the modern psychological novel, the hero is abnormal. The center is not central. You can make a story out of a hero among dragons but not out of a dragon among dragons. The fairy tale discusses what a sane man will do in a mad world.

G. K. CHESTERTON

Our experience of the world has two parts, the sacred and the mundane. The division between the two is not always clear, nor easily understood. But understanding the difference can help us reconcile the two.

The food-gathering method of the Trobriand Islanders illustrates our different approaches to the two realms. The Trobrianders live on atolls off the eastern coast of New Guinea in the southwest Pacific. Most of their food comes from fishing in the protected Trobriand lagoon. They use traditional fishing methods there, and an abundant catch, for which the Trobrianders are regularly thankful to their gods, is usually assured. On exceptional occasions, however, fishing on the open seas becomes necessary. The Trobrianders' tiny boats don't fare so well in the heavy waves. Danger can strike quickly from seas roiled by sudden storms. Because of the hazards, elaborate rituals and magic rites to appease angry gods are performed before the islanders venture forth.[1]

Our experience of prayer is similar in some ways to the Trobriander's fishing preferences. Most of our prayer takes place in the lagoons of life. We live in the everyday. Our experiences of God usually come from familiar events: a child's loving touch, a mate's caress, the satisfaction of steady Christian growth. Most of our spiritual sustenance comes from this common, faithful source. Occasionally, circumstances or desire force us to leap into the supernatural realm, and God descends to meet us in a special way. It is a meeting laden with all the drama, derring-do, and indeed, danger of a Moses meeting God on Mount Sinai. "Who shall look on the face of God and live?" Thankfully, most of our prayer takes place in the lagoon; thankfully, we live most of our lives by the rules of the ordinary.

To say that we live and pray by the rules of the ordinary does not demean their value. God answers simple as well as elaborate prayers. Heartfelt requests, regularly voiced, reach God as quickly and easily as emergency calls breathed in the midst of flames. Ordinary prayers from ordinary people are answered with extraordinary power.

Further, there are distinct advantages to ordinary prayer. Since it is part of daily living, ordinary prayer follows the rules of the habitual. The same forces that shape our lives shape our prayers. If we are tired, prayer is difficult. If we are energized, prayer comes more easily. Daily events and our own psychological make-up affect our prayer life a great deal.

In one sense, this fact of the ordinary is a limitation. It makes the ideal prayer life—what Paul called ceaseless prayer—almost impossible. Few in history have attained the state of perfectly reconciling the natural and the supernatural. Christ did. Perhaps Enoch, who the Bible says was in constant touch with God.[2] His reward was to circumvent death. But few of us can realistically hope for that kind of prayer relationship. We live with the reality of our humanness.

Jim Davey, pastor of a Christian and Missionary Alliance church in Seattle, Washington, compared his prayer life to seeing Mount Rainier, which at times dominates the horizon of the Seattle area. "On a very few days out of the year, Mount Rainier is visible to us. On most days it isn't. It's shrouded by clouds, haze, and mist. My prayer life is like that. Several times each year I see and love God clearly, in an especially profound way. On most days, however, I pray out of desperation, need, or blind faith. Without a simple, mundane commitment to pray, I would skip it."

Davey's analogy rings true. Leaders who have coped have learned to look for God in the ordinary not the extraordinary. The deepest religious experiences don't keep the appointments set for them by self-styled dispensers of satisfaction. God cannot be staged nor prayer scripted. Instead, God comes when we least expect him, when we so enthrall ourselves in the business of being Christian that our seeking self no longer blocks the way.

Leaders talked about finding God in three ordinary areas of life:

The Ordinaries of Culture

Dozens of currently published books show how modern society has given itself over to secularization and humanism. The arguments are similar, and a composite on prayer might read as follows: *We live in a culture that discourages prayer. We are a mechanized, secularized society. We are surrounded by appliances that satisfy our every culinary need, home entertainment devices that stimulate our senses both good and bad, transportation possibilities that take the sting out of travel, and working tools that make labor a misnomer. This ease of satisfying want and whim is what makes prayer so difficult. Prayer, the essence of which is obedience and submission, runs counter to a culture where we are beholden to very few. Further, some cultures in history have revolved around the church and the monastery. Ours doesn't. We live in a secular culture where man, not God, is the measure of all things.*[3]

This is a convincing argument—partly because it's true. Even Christian leaders feel the effects of secularization and its discouraging effects on prayer. One pastor said: "I am currently serving my first call, and have been in the parish two years. I get the feeling others don't think my personal devotional life is important. Perhaps they assume I have a strong spiritual inner life. But in my two years here, not one person has asked me about the health of my personal faith. I feel unsupported in this aspect of my life. It's as if it didn't matter to the job I do here."

It would be easy to uncritically accept the common wisdom that our society is so secularized that prayer is almost impossible. However, if religious history has anything to teach us about cultural conditions conducive to prayer, we may be in a time of unparalleled opportunity.

Consider an example from the history of Islam. Researcher George Koovackal notes that Muhammad made prayer a central feature of Islam because it was particularly suited to the nomadic life. He recognized it would be very difficult to maintain orthodoxy among a people completely decentralized by their wandering existence. So he made the external forms of the faith of central importance. A Muslim can walk into an Islamic community in a totally different culture and immediately recognize Islamic faith by its five traditional pillars: prayer five times daily, profession of faith, almsgiving, pilgrimage, and fasting. Commitment to prayer and devotional practice become vitally important in an atmosphere of uncertainty and change.[4]

We find ourselves in a similar atmosphere today. We are not dependent on wandering flocks, moveable tents, and watering holes. But our wealth, changing industries, and fragmented culture have made us technological nomads. Few of us live in one house for more than five years. Fewer still stay in one job that long. Spiritually, a bewildering variety of denominations and factions within denominations create an insecurity about the content of our faith. When we walk into a strange church, we don't know what to expect. We thirst for some kind of quality control in our religious organizations. This need is especially compelling when we see the flourishing of cults and new religious movements that supply this kind of security.

Viewed this way, a culture that temporalizes organization, depersonalizes fraternity, and homogenizes individuality forces even religion to be distilled to its essence—for the

Christian the man/God relationship. Our renewed interest in Christian spirituality is a sign that devotional practice can supply needed stability in the face of diversity. In some ways, secularization is presenting unique opportunities to the Christian's prayer life.

Perhaps the Christian leader's strategy in the face of secularization is to use it to advantage. The truth of prayer hasn't changed. But the way we gain access to it needs modification. Jean-Pierre de Caussade, in a delightful book, *Sacrament of the Present Moment,* said: "God still speaks today as he spoke to our forefathers in days gone by. The spiritual life then was a matter of immediate communication with God. It had not been reduced to a fine art nor was lofty and detailed guidance to it provided with a wealth of rules, instructions, and maxims. These may very well be necessary today. But it was not so in those early days, when people were more direct and unsophisticated."[5]

Are people less direct and more sophisticated today? The point is arguable. But *times* have changed. The pressures of an informational age are enormous. We have literally hundreds of things to do and thousands of suggestions on how to do them. We live in an age when ordinary habits have become essential. Al Ries and Jack Trout recently wrote a book called *Positioning: The Battle for Your Mind,* in which they paint the following picture: Western man's mind is like a sponge oversaturated with information. It is dripping full, and a lukewarm message or a message given only once will not penetrate that sponge—it will trickle off with the rest. Only that which is repeated or presented in such a way to make it stick will stay with us.[6]

People who pray must learn regular patterns of behavior. Without habits, schedules squeeze and word blizzards obscure the best of intentions. In developing a habit of prayer, we can utilize the ordinaries of our secularized culture instead of fighting them. For example, we can use:

• the beauty of art. One pastor pointed to a painting on his study wall and said, "For some reason, when I look at that painting, I'm reminded of God and my need to pray. It triggers short ten-minute periods of prayer throughout my day."

• the intensely individualistic self-help techniques so popular now. Prayer lists, prayer partners, memory techniques all can be aided and refined by self-help hints.

• retreat centers and beautiful natural settings have never been more available. The ease with which we can travel to such mind-stretching locales make them real aids to prayer.

• the fitness craze. Many Christian leaders admit they pray when they jog, ride exercise bicycles, or hike in the woods.

By maintaining our spiritual center in God, cultural fad and fashion can aid prayer life without fear of compromising our spiritual needs and eccentricities. Even humanistic culture can become an ally.

The Ordinaries of Our Minds

God created each person's mind to be unique. But in spite of this uniqueness, behavior patterns are remarkably consistent from human being to human being. One of the common patterns is that persistent, consistent repetition of an act affects both the actor and those acted upon. In a familiar parable, Jesus showed how that principle extends to prayer:

A widow, he said, who had been wronged by another person, went to a judge for relief. The judge was an evil man. He would not give the woman relief on the merits of her case, just as he made few decisions on moral grounds. Yet the widow was persistent. Every day she came to the judge's courtroom to plead her case. Finally, out of exasperation at her constant coming, the judge ruled in her favor. Jesus used the story (Luke 18) to illustrate the need for habitual prayer. Our relief before God will come not on the merits of our case (for who among us can say we *deserve* relief?) but only out of our constant requests for God's grace.

Jesus isn't arguing for mindless repetition of prayers. He's asking for persistence. (Traditionally, theologians have called it importunity.) Put simply, developing a consistent prayer life requires the will to do it.

One way to buttress the will required is to develop a habit of praying. Not a habit that leads to mindless repetition, but a discipline that intensifies and deepens our prayer experience. Psychologist William James called habit "the enormous fly-wheel of society," the element that holds everything together.[7] Habits make most things predictable and reliable. We can handle the exceptional and the creative only because we have the habitual as a backdrop.

It is a backdrop that can be learned. Richard Foster, in *Celebration of Discipline*, says that prayer is not an innate skill, but something we learn to do. "One of the liberating experiences of my life came when I understood that prayer involved a learning process. I was set free to question, to experiment, even to fail, for I knew I was learning."[8] Foster illustrates with the example of a television set. If we turn on the television and it doesn't work, we do not automatically assume TVs don't exist. We fix it. So with prayer. If our prayers are not working properly, if we cannot get ourselves to pray regularly, we must do something to fix the problem, not dismiss prayer as an unreal, mystical, or impossible endeavor.

Ordinary habits and techniques are important in helping us take advantage of the mind's receptivity to discipline. Much of the Christian leader's behavior in the various ministry functions is determined by them. Take teaching for example. Psychologist Dan Landis made a study of classroom teachers to try to determine how much of their teaching behavior was determined by habit and how much was consciously thought-out behavior. Both verbal and nonverbal behaviors were measured. By observing and recording teaching styles in classroom settings, he discovered that more behavior was performed out of habit than volition. Teaching style quickly became second nature and freed teachers to focus on content and subtle points of pedagogy.[9]

Similarly, the more of our praying we can make habitual, the more we can work on refining and improving it. If we can make the fact of our going to prayer so ordinary that we don't have to use a great deal of energy to force ourselves to our knees each and every time, then we can focus on prayer requests and deepen the quality of our time with God.

The Ordinaries of Ministry

Is it possible to be a professional prayer leader and a devout person of prayer at the same time? Church leaders help parishioners enrich their prayer lives—does that stifle their own? Church leaders lead corporate prayer in public services—does that inhibit their own participation? Church leaders set up prayer chains, prayer vigils, and prayer meetings—does that make prayer a program instead of a worship experience for the leader?

Some don't think so. William Law, in *A Practical Treatise Upon Christian Perfection*, talks about the dangers of professional Christianity. Suppose, Law says, you were to call a man from a sumptuous feast. You tell him to go into the next room and be hungry for a half hour; then he can go back to feasting. He might obey you by going into the hunger room. He might even sit there licking his lips for a half hour. But the man is not really hungry. Why not? Because he has just come from a feast and his appetite is dull.[10]

Do church leaders run the risk of dull appetites because of the continuous availability of spiritual food? Many leaders admit the problem. Yet several said the very opposite can happen. The tasks of ministry can feed the minister's prayer life. They need not always be separated. Lynn Kent, pastor of the Greater Portland (Oregon) Bible Church, finds his prayer life tied closely to his preaching:

"I respond to God from the text I'm preaching on each week. I've heard pastors say they keep their prayer life separate from sermon preparation, but I combine the two. I want to preach the truth of each passage. To do so, I must discover the mind of God as much as I am able. Prayer helps me do that. The heart of my prayer life is responding to the Word."

Prayer is a vital part of the Christian leader's life. One way to look at that importance is the negative. Charles Finney once advised a young ministerial student: "If you lose your spirit of prayer, you will do nothing, or next to nothing, even if you have the intellectual endowment of an angel. If you lose your spirituality, you had better go about some other employment, for I cannot contemplate a more loathsome object than an earthly-minded minister."[11]

What Finney said is quite true. However, there is also a positive approach. The everyday occurrences of ministry are ideal opportunities for prayer and communion with God. No one is more ideally situated to cultivate the spiritual life than the Christian leader who approaches his or her charges with eyes open for God's wonder-working grace.

When that expectancy of grace is present and when the physical fact of prayer is established, it sometimes surprises us how it comes alive when needed. God will work powerfully through the ordinary tasks of ministry, even in routine prayer. Jim Davey remembers a particularly striking instance:

"In a former pastorate in Burlington, Vermont, the six hundred church members were evenly divided about whether or not to relocate. For seven years we had struggled with the question. The issue was raised anew when six acres of prime property became available just down the street. I called a meeting of the board.

"We met on Saturday morning. Since we knew the real division on the board, fueled by seven years of controversy, we agreed to stay until we reached agreement. Then we prayed. We always started our meetings with prayer, but I'm not sure we thought the prayer was that important to what we were really going to do that morning. Each of us prayed aloud and asked God for guidance.

"As soon as we finished praying, the sixteen of us looked at one another and knew we should buy the land. By 11:30 the meeting was over. That may not sound like much. But if I could tell you the intensity of disagreement over this issue that had preceded that meeting, and the warmth of agreement that followed, you'd be as shocked as I was at what happened.

"What happened? While we prayed God gave us his mind. The prayer was a customary, perfunctory act perhaps. But through it God told us what to do."

Spurred by bigger than life expectations, society has added the prefix "super" to words like star, hero, and market. Christians gullibly followed suit with superchurch, superpastor, and superspiritual. But the intent of highlighting high performance is rarely successful. Usually the result is a devaluing of the root word and a grimacing embarrassment over the super-compound.

Super-prayer? Ironically, prayer, like life itself, only becomes "super" when surrounded by humility, commonness, and the ordinary acceptance of a love beyond comprehension.

THREE

THE VARIETY OF PRACTICE

True prayer is not to be found in the words of the mouth, but in the thoughts of the heart.

GREGORY THE GREAT

To generalize is to be an idiot.

WILLIAM BLAKE

F

our of us sat at breakfast not long ago. Two of my companions were pastors; the third was a new Christian trying to quit smoking. As he lit up his fourth post-breakfast cigarette, he commented: "Quitting smoking is as hard as trying to develop a prayer life. I've been trying to do that lately, too. Do you guys have any suggestions on how to establish a regular prayer life?"

Asking two pastors for spiritual counsel is like asking an insurance agent about pension plans. Paul took the lead:

"I've struggled for twenty years with a need for regularity and consistency in my prayer life. I longed for an intense, quality time with the Lord. The image that kept running through my mind was that of Adam meeting the Lord in the cool of the day.

"In an attempt to achieve that, I tried particularly hard to get up early in the morning for prayer. It didn't work for me. About five years ago I finally said, 'Lord, I can't handle this problem. If you want me to pray regularly, show me how to do it.'

"About that time I started waking up at two or three in the morning. Without any reason I would suddenly be wide awake. At first I didn't realize what was happening. I thought I might be ill. After three consecutive nights of this, I decided if

I couldn't go back to sleep, I'd try praying. It was some of the most meaningful prayer I had ever experienced. I felt God was there in the room with me. Now I wake up in the middle of almost every night and pray for thirty to ninety minutes. Then I fall back to sleep. That's how the Lord answered my prayer about personal time with him."

Gordon listened respectfully. Although he was as impressed with Paul's discovery as we were, he had a different experience:

"I, too, struggled with personal prayer early in my ministry. My wife and I wanted desperately to serve God as best we could, and we did everything we could think of to make our first churches all they could be. We worked hard. But after several years I realized I was getting by on natural ability and sooner or later my lack of a quiet time with God would catch up with me—I'd find myself totally dry.

"But the Lord worked differently in my life than he did in Paul's. I decided I'd try to get up at 5 A.M. and pray and do Bible study for one hour. I started setting my alarm clock ten minutes earlier and earlier each day until I was getting up at five. I soon found I thrived on the spiritual food I was getting in that hour of quiet. Once I got started, I felt like I had an appointment with God every morning, and I couldn't wait to meet him. I have never quit the practice. It's an invariable in my schedule now."

Two radically different approaches to prayer. One gives it up to the unknown guidance of the Holy Spirit, the other to a disciplined, regimented approach utilizing the Spirit's power. Yet both are committed men of God, if the many fruits of their respective ministries are any indication. Which style is right? Which is the model to follow?

Perhaps neither. Or maybe both. If talking to Christian leaders revealed one thing, it was there are many different ways to pray with effective spiritual power. One of the difficulties in talking about prayer practices is that there is no single correct way.

Leaders said they became comfortable with prayer only when they finally realized they were unique and had to do it in a way that fit them. One said: "I've come to a degree of peace about my prayer life and what God expects. I'm sure my prayer could be more effective, but I don't feel guilty about it. When I see people who do, I get a little bit worried. It's as if we're not measuring up to the standard, but the standard we're getting is not from God's Word, but from the extraordinary examples of prayer. Let's face it. The people who write books don't have ordinary experiences, and yet they're the ones who create the level of expectations.

"I remember trying to spend long periods of time in prayer at a former church. That church was started by a man renowned for the hours he spent on his knees. Having that kind of model around can really put a load of guilt on you. I remember worrying about the poverty of my own prayer life. I'd get into my office resolved to pray for hours. But it just wasn't me, and I couldn't do it."

Prayer styles seem to fall into two main camps. On the one hand are the disciplined saints determined to build their faith through prayer no matter what the cost. On the other hand are the faithful who trust God will call them to their knees whenever he deems it necessary. Interestingly, these two ends of what really is a long spectrum of practice (no one is fully one or the other) correspond to two main philosophical theories of how virtues are developed.

Aristotle felt virtues were innate human possibilities that are only awaiting the development of the appropriate skills to be put into practice. Translation: When you develop the skills to pray, you will pray and your faith will grow.

Plato felt that people would naturally act virtuously if they fully understood what the virtue in question was. Lack of skill is not the problem, lack of understanding is. Translation: If you fully understand why it is important to pray, then you will naturally pray.

Of course, neither Aristotle nor Plato were talking about

Christian faith and prayer.[1] But their categories and arguments are remarkably similar to the question raised about whether faith or the practice of prayer comes first. In order to more fully examine the question, let's look at an example of each prayer style. To explore the implications, we will look at a Christian leader who demonstrates each style. Naturally, we are using them only as illustrations and are not commenting on the motives that have driven them to use this style.

The Disciplined Way

After teaching theology in a Christian college for several years, John Piper became pastor of Bethlehem Baptist Church in Minneapolis, Minnesota, a center-city church of three hundred fifty. The church has grown to a Sunday morning attendance of seven hundred thirty. Piper attributes the growth to an intensely God-centered worship service.

An intense person, Piper speaks with a wiry toughness that typifies his approach to ministry. He reads Jonathan Edwards with a passion, and, following Edwards's claim to be a "God-besotted man," he has told his church his desire for them is to be a "God-besotted church."

In his devotional time, John is a systematic pray-er. He gets up a half hour before his four children and his wife, Noel, and he uses that time to prepare himself before God for the stresses of early morning family life and for the family devotions after breakfast.

"I found I had to 'get my own heart happy before God' before I could effectively lead my family in devotions," he says. "That phrase is from George Mueller who said he discovered early in his life that if he got up early and tried to read and pray, his mind would always wander. So instead he would just say, 'Lord, open my eyes to see wonderful things out of your law,' and then he began reading Scripture until he got his heart happy in the Lord. He wouldn't see anyone until that happened.

"After leading the kids in a devotional after breakfast and

getting them off to school, I read the newspaper and return to my study. I don't go to the church until noon. In my study I have a prayer bench, and I kneel there and roll my concerns onto the Lord. That again is from George Mueller who had a mental image of one by one rolling all of his concerns onto the Lord each morning. Then later in the day when the world might be coming down around his head, he had the calmness of knowing that all his cares were in God's hands. I mentally think through the day to come and roll each and every task onto God.

"I have already prayed for my family before and during breakfast; my next priority is my staff and key volunteers at church. Then I pray for the congregation. I systematically go through the church directory. Next I work on a prayer list of missions concerns, local concerns, and other individuals. Then I read the Bible. Recently, I have used McCheyne's method of reading the Old Testament once each year and the New Testament twice. It's basically about four chapters a day, and I proceed slowly because I mingle prayer with my reading. After that I'm ready for study, sermon preparation, and later the work at church.

"Noel and I end the day with evening prayer together and often read to each other aloud from a book for fifteen minutes. It's amazing how much reading you can do that way. We've found we read fifteen to twenty books a year if we are consistent."

Piper's prayer life represents that of many pastors who structure their time carefully, using the discipline to ensure they get in the time needed. Most cautioned against confusing their method with the real heart of prayer. Piper cited Matthew 6 (praying in secret) as a warning against setting up anyone's prayer practice as normative.

Those who use this kind of approach, though, can point to Hebrews 5 as ample justification for their disciplined time. The writer recommends the solid food of the gospel only for the mature "who by constant use have trained themselves to distinguish good from evil." Salvation is not enough to develop this ability; one needs to seek maturity by honing the skills of discernment.

There are several different directions this approach to prayer practice can take us. On the one hand, it can feed into a strong mystical tradition. Mysticism stresses that spiritual maturity is attained in graduated stages. In this tradition, the discipline of spiritual habits is only the beginning stage that leads on to higher things. For example, St. John of the Ladder, a seventh-century mystic, identified four stages of spiritual development, comparing them to rungs of a ladder stretching upward to perfection. The first rung is to tame the passions, the second to pray with the lips, the third is to practice inner prayer, and the fourth is to rise seeing visions. The habit of prayer deals with the first two rungs, leading to the third, and perhaps, if you're a mystic, the fourth.[2]

Or the disciplined approach can lead to a simplified way to promote evangelism. Blaise Pascal's well-known "wager" is an example. The French philosopher said that in all matters of faith, including prayer, you cannot "prove" God is at work— but it is well worth the wager. You cannot prove prayer will be meaningful, but Pascal's advice to believers is: The *practice* of the religious life will put your belief on a firmer psychological basis.

Deed leads to thought: "For we must make no mistake about ourselves: we are as much automaton as mind. As a result, demonstration is not the only instrument for convincing us. How few things can be demonstrated. Proofs only convince the mind; habit provides the strongest proofs and those that are most believed. . . . When we believe only by the strength of our conviction and the automaton is inclined to believe the opposite, that is not enough. We must therefore make both parts of us believe: the mind by reasons, which need to be seen only once in a lifetime, and the automaton by habit, and not allowing it any inclination to the contrary."[3]

The best argument for the disciplined approach to prayer is simply that, for whatever reason, it does lead to increased, deepened faith. Martin Luther frequently mentioned it. In his

Treatise on Good Works, he talks about the value of habit to developing firmer faith. In his discussion of the second commandment, he notes a common complaint he heard from Christians: *I don't have much faith that my prayers will be heard—so I don't pray.*

Luther's response? "That's the very reason you should pray. God commands us to pray so that we can find out what we can and cannot do. Even if we begin with a very weak spark of faith, we must pray daily so the weak spark is fanned through regular exercise into a full flame of faith."[4]

Luther goes on to say that weak faith is not a sign of weak Christians. Even the apostles, including Peter, prayed for increased faith. Indeed, prayer should be seen not as a good work, but as a means to increasing our faith. That can only be done through regular, habitual prayer.

And on the modern front we can only say that it works. Testimonies such as John Piper's are common. So is the behavioral evidence of what prayer can do. L. D. Nelson and Russell Dynes reported in a research article in the *Journal for the Scientific Study of Religion* that people who attended church frequently and performed other acts of devotion (such as prayer) had higher rates of helping behavior than those who didn't.[5] Apparently devotionalism has a positive influence on the way people live out their faith. As Aristotle said in his *Ethics*, "We become just by performing just acts, temperate by performing temperate ones, brave by performing brave ones." Might we extrapolate and say we become men and women of prayer by praying, not by thinking about prayer and hoping it comes?

The Haphazardly Intent Way

Bud Palmberg is pastor of Mercer Island Covenant Church in Mercer Island, Washington, one of the wealthiest areas surrounding Seattle. A large man, he commands attention by his physical presence as much as through his insights. He speaks colorfully, Van Dyke beard bobbing with each freshly crafted metaphor. The span of his ministry is what impresses. He's a small town Nebraska boy who still wears cowboy boots as he ministers to well-to-dos in Mercer Island, including business executives, Seattle Seahawks football players, and attorneys. But one night each week he cruises the streets of skid-row Seattle presenting the gospel to prostitutes and motorcycle gangs in a program called Operation Nightwatch he started with other Seattle pastors.

Palmberg describes his prayer as the "style of a driven pastor." He prays on the run.

"Prayer is my primary back-up system. The longer I'm in ministry, the more I realize that prayer is like respiration. It's my deep breaths between appointments, my sighs when I feel down, my gasps when I'm in trouble. I try to make prayer the backdrop to everything else I do.

"Why don't I lock myself in my closet every morning? Because I can't sit still that long. And I've found that you can pray while you're walking. Or, if you live on an island like we do, while you're sitting in your car waiting for traffic to clear on the bridge to the mainland. My walk with God is comfortable enough for me that I don't feel the need for a formalized place or time or structure for my prayer. In the morning I hit the road running and I try to have an open channel to God all the time. I don't want to have to dial God—I can just say, 'Help me, God,' or 'Thank you, Lord,' or 'That's fantastic,' whenever something strikes me.

"As I pray in those short snatches throughout the day I always try and have a notebook near because as I pray I'm reminded of needs people have: 'I haven't seen him lately,' or 'She was considering surgery last week. I wonder how she's doing?' or 'How's that family coping?' I also try to read in short snatches, and I've found the Psalms to be my greatest resource for prayer-oriented reading. The Psalms are the blueprints of prayer.

"My prayer style fits my conception of ministry. Frankly, I'm over my head most of the time. I'm treading water administratively. I have a congregation that can dance circles around me in organizational skills. There are saints in this church that dwarf me spiritually. The only thing I have going for me is I'm willing to take it all on and be responsible for it. That's a real incentive for prayer."

Palmberg believes the ministry is ideally suited for "informed" prayer. "Because of the nature of my job, I know more about people than anyone else. What a golden opportunity to pray specifically for needs. The first free minute I have after I leave someone, I pray a short prayer for them and their problems. That's something I don't know at five o'clock in the morning but I do right after I leave someone. I believe God honors specific prayers. That advantage of knowing a great deal has become a responsibility, an impetus to passionate praying for me.

"I know pastors I highly respect who practice very structured prayer. But whenever I try it I've felt terribly self-righteous. I already have enough trouble with that, so I gave up trying to structure my prayer life."

You don't have to talk very long to Palmberg to realize that his lack of structure doesn't translate to a lack of prayer. Others in the church testify to the power of his public prayers and many can cite instances of private prayer sessions with their pastor that have led to serendipitous answers and spiritual growth. By all indicators, Palmberg's prayer life doesn't lack power, just structure.

Many pastors follow Palmberg's style. They are generally too activist in personality to sit still for any length of time when there's ministry to be done. Yet their personalities and strong faith drive them to prayer and the resulting power they need for ministry. The Bible is clear that this relationship between prayer and power is invariable. In Matthew 17 Jesus heals a mentally deranged boy whose sickness often made him fall in the fire or water. The boy's father brought him to Jesus after first bringing him to the disciples. The disciples failed in their attempts to heal him.

After seeing the illness cured at Jesus' command, the disciples asked him why they had failed. After all, they had been able to cure in other situations. Jesus lays the blame at the disciples' feet. Because of their lack of faith, he says, they didn't have the power to heal this particularly stubborn case. Faith is like the potential power represented in the water trapped behind a dam. In order to be made useful as electricity, it must be funneled into a conduit that will turn the generator's blades. Prayer is like that conduit, turning the potential of faith given as grace into wonder-working power that can change the world.

Christian leaders like Bud Palmberg feel free to call on God through prayer whenever a task of ministry or personal living requires it. The faith is there—it only needs activating through prayer. More than that though, they have developed a prayer style that relies on the incidents and difficulties of life to call them to prayer. If life and our relationship to God is fully understood, prayer is a natural way of behaving.

Calvin credits faith with all answers to prayer and with driving us to our knees in prayer. After citing Romans 10:14— "How, then, can they call on the one they have not believed in?"—he goes on to say that "faith gets whatever is granted to prayer."[6] For Calvin, faith, saving faith at least, is the necessary foundation for all prayer.

For the haphazardly intent, prayer is the overflowing of a heart longing for intimacy with a personal God. Paul Rees, traveling lecturer for World Vision International, talks about prayer as relationship, not discipline: "There is biblical justification for referring to prayer at times as real discipline. Paul speaks about Epaphras as one who labored in prayer. But prayer is a relationship so intimate and so dynamic that it should be easy to listen for God's voice and to respond by articulating some confession or petition. This idea of prayer as a relationship has grown on me through the years, so that now for me prayer is the healthy expression of this intimacy with God."

One of the values of stressing haphazardly intent prayer is the lessening of negative incentives. We don't pray because we have to, but because we love God so much we feel we must. Henri Nouwen talked about the problem Christian leaders sometimes have in making time for prayer. Nouwen identified with that problem, but suggested something he had found helpful: "I can't fight the demons of distraction directly. I can't say *No* to television, or *No* to my overcrowded schedule unless there is something ten times more attractive pulling me away. The only thing I know of that is ten times more attractive than the lure of creaturely comforts is to be loved with God's love, either directly or through one of his followers. If I can experience God's love in my brokenness, I become free from the compulsions of doing anything—but then I want to do everything for him."

Prayer is not drudgery that must be performed in order to satisfy some divine taskmaster snapping a whip over our cracking knees and furrowed brow. Instead, acceptance of God's love leads to prayer.

Prayer and Faith Feed on Each Other

Both Piper and Palmberg are men of prayer. Recognizing the varieties of prayer does not mean we decide one style is better than another. We could line up witnesses to disciplined prayer, pair them with witnesses to the haphazardly intent approach, and come out just about even.

And it would be foolish to try to reconcile them in one theory of "true and valid prayer," as if that were possible. Both styles are true and valid, although based perhaps on different premises. How the Holy Spirit works in lives is an intensely individual thing. Even distinguishing only two categories of prayer practice is overly simplistic.

Indeed, one of the attractions of studying prayer is the many different forms it can take in the lives of Christian leaders. Trying to define orthodox prayer practice too narrowly and uniformly can gloss over the remarkable ways God's grace works in different lives.

It is also possible that one person can use several different styles. Cassian reports that in Egypt in the fourth century, the elders of the Christian church prescribed the prayer norm to be followed by the monks: "Twelve Psalms for an evening Office and the same number for a night Office. The presumption was that during the day each monk arranged in his own way for prayer and words of Scripture to accompany his manual work."[7] In effect this combines formal hours of prayer with personalized structure, whatever that may be.

In reality, we all need the fruits of both approaches. Some may need more of one than the other. But the *truths* of both must be recognized by all Christians. Andrew Murray in his classic book on prayer, *With Christ in the School of Prayer*, said that "faith needs a life of prayer for its full growth."[8] Perhaps that, after all, is the best statement of the relationship between the two. There is value in viewing the relationship between prayer and faith in both priority sequences: faith leads to prayer, and prayer increases faith. Both are indispensable. Some incipient faith must be present to stimulate the believer to want to pray, to take advantage of the power God offers through his Holy Spirit in order to allow us to pray. However, prayer increases faith, and anything we can do to foster the habit of prayer will be valuable.

The habit of prayer will lead to a oneness of spirit with God. Our motivations to prayer may not be pure as we begin. They may be naive, misguided, even cynical. But regular prayer and sincere effort to understand prayer will change that. As Sören Kierkegaard noted, "The immediate person thinks and imagines that when he prays, the important thing, the thing he must concentrate upon, is that God should hear what he is praying for. And yet, in the true, eternal sense, it is just the reverse. The true relation in prayer is not when God hears what is prayed for, but when the person praying continues to pray until he is the one who hears, who hears what God wills. The immediate person therefore uses many words, and therefore makes demands in his prayer. The true man of prayer only attends."[9]

Developing a prayer style that fits your needs requires two things. First you must clearly see the *purpose* of prayer—why a

Christian must pray. Primary motivation is essential. Second, you must solve the *process* to go through in order to make regular prayer a reality.

F O U R

IS PRAYER A MUST?

God's command and promise is our sole motive for prayer. Nothing could be commanded more precisely than what is stated in the Psalm, 'Call upon me in the day of tribulation' (50:15). Those who try to wriggle out of coming directly to God are not only rebellious and stubborn, but are also convicted of unbelief because they distrust the promises.

JOHN CALVIN

Prayer is the sincere, sensible, affectionate pouring out of the heart or soul to God through Christ in the strength and assistance of the Holy Spirit, for such things as God hath promised, or according to the Word for the good of the church, with submission and faith to the will of God.

JOHN BUNYAN

What drives us to prayer? One pastor said, "It's a little bit like loving your wife: you love her for a variety of reasons, and different reasons predominate at different times. Sometimes you pray out of sheer desperation. Sometimes out of unhappiness with yourself. Sometimes because you love the Lord. Sometimes it's a sense of feeling utterly overwhelmed—a feeling of inadequacy. A person will call on the phone and say, 'My wife just kicked me out of the house. Can I come over and talk with you?' So you'll say, 'Sure, come on over and we'll talk.' You hang up the phone, and say to yourself, *What in the world do I say to this person?* That's when you pray."

That kind of pressure can drive the Christian leader in one of two directions: toward spiritual arrogance or toward total dependence on God. When the pressure is handled with simplistic authoritarianism ("I'm the only one who can handle this situation"), the leader is susceptible to arrogance. The road to that extreme leads to burnout or becoming hardened by spiritual callousness.

The road to total dependence, however, is a difficult one. It is relatively easy to drop to one's knees in emergency situations; it is much more difficult to depend on God when things are going well. The prayers of contrition uttered when things are going well, however, are the signs of true dependence on God. What are the forces that should drive us to our knees in the good times?

There are many good reasons to pray, but only one rises above the vicissitudes of life, above the vagaries of the emotional roller coaster we ride daily. That primary reason should head the list.

Obedience

God commands us to pray. Faithful followers obey that command. Unfortunately, obedience is not the most popular motivation today. It is certainly not an act that men and women in leadership positions are accustomed to performing. Obedience requires a loss of freedom. In human situations it means entrusting part of our will to someone else. In the divine situation it means entrusting our total will to God.

Leaders do not feel comfortable entrusting their wills to someone else. Ordinarily, leaders rise to their positions of responsibility because they make good decisions. Whether their skills are entrepreneurial or managerial, the levers of decision making feel good in their hands. A certain level of independence is required of those who shoulder the loneliness of leadership. Used to the freedom, leaders are usually reluctant obeyers.

This does not mean Christian leaders are bad Christians. On the contrary, they are often very effective because they choose to operate on the basis of another command of God, the Great Commandment, which says to love God totally and to love our neighbors as we love ourselves. Effective leaders do not submit to self-destructive employees, power-grabbing associates, or advisers of limited vision. Effective leaders do, however, constantly put the welfare of each of these groups above even their own welfare, and make decisions accordingly—not necessarily giving each group what it wants, but what it needs. That's operating by the command of love.

If we could consistently operate on the basis of this commandment, both in relation to colleagues and to God, the problem with prayer would be solved. If our love for human beings were perfect, all our personnel decisions would be effective ones. If our love for God were perfect, we would desire constant communion with him. Prayer would be a way of life.

Unfortunately, few of us are able to claim perfect love. Clouds of one sort or another hide our vision of God far more days than we would like to admit. We want to do the best for those around us, but our pride and self-interest keep tripping us up. We can't love perfectly because our love for ourselves keeps getting in the way. Thus we are thrown back to depend on the law of obedience. We do what God commands. Given our sinful human natures, it's a more reliable guide.

The religions of the world have long recognized the need for the law of obedience to compensate for our inability to love perfectly. Judaism, for example, has a tradition regarding the many items of its law code. Rabbis call it the "fence around the law."[1] Only a small percentage of those laws are absolutely essential to avoid apostasy. The others are important, however, because they act as buffers to keep the faithful from breaking the core laws.

In truth, for the average religious person, these peripheral laws become as important as the core laws because they define a lifestyle that should become second nature. They live that way not out of following the law but because they love God. But, life being what it is, very few can live a faithful lifestyle out of love. So God commands it through the law.

Christianity has a similar tradition. We have our "negative" standards about what it means to be a Christian, such as the Ten Commandments. I grew up with an additional Baptist fence around the law: Thou shalt not smoke, drink, dance, play cards, watch television, or play baseball on Sunday. In truth, following these "laws" is not necessary to being a Christian. But I followed them and reflect on them with fondness. The content of those laws did not make me a better Christian; the act of obeying them probably did.

Depending upon our stage of Christian maturity, our obedience can be done out of varying degrees of love or be done strictly mechanically. Christian mystics, such as Theophan the Recluse, valued unquestioning obedience above any ascetic feat: "You have termed unwilling obedience 'mechanical obedience.' In actual fact, the only kind of obedience that effectively shapes our character is obedience performed against our own will and our own ideas. If you do something because that is the way your heart is inclined, where is the obedience? You are merely following your own will and tastes. If you recognize your motives, you make such self-willed action slightly better. But in true obedience you obey without seeing the reason for what you are told to do, and in spite of your own reluctance."[2]

Although it does risk the danger of mechanical observance, obedience has advantages: It is simple, and there is less chance to subconsciously fail in obeying than in loving. It's no secret that the minute we try to do something good out of our own efforts, it begins to be mixed with pride and selfishness. Obedience and submission to God minimize that pride, although we can never do away with it completely.

For this reason, obedience is the primary reason we should pray. God commands it, and a command from God implies a relationship with the commander. We obey because we are loyal to our leader, and we want to comply. We pray to obey.

Dissecting Obedience

Our minds being what they are, the simple command of obedience does not satisfy us intellectually. Although it is reason enough to force us on our knees, obedience can leave us cold when the everyday emotions of anger, frustration, depression, and desire seem to control our every move.

Obedience insures that we come to God in prayer, but it cannot prepare us emotionally to seek God. Each time we come we have different feelings about our purpose. We may come with a heart overwhelmed with God's goodness. We may come angry that his faithful servants are being mistreated. We may come wishing to confess our sin. We may come with requests for ourselves or others. Each of these is a valid motivation for prayer. Each helps determine the content of a particular prayer. Each, if understood, can help us structure our prayer time more effectively.

There is another very practical reason for looking beyond obedience for more specific motivations. Understanding why we pray (or don't pray) is the first step toward establishing the habit of prayer.[3] Understanding motives is important, and we need to check those motives against what God expects of us in prayer. The techniques for developing consistent habits work if the will to use them is present. But the will to adopt them comes from understanding God's context for prayer.

Richard "Doc" Kirk, youth pastor of River Road Baptist Church in Eugene, Oregon, found that his lifelong desire for understanding and wisdom has been the motive for his prayer life: "My biblical hero has always been Solomon. Ever since I was a teenager, I have asked God for wisdom because that was what Solomon had. I remember a particular incident that convinced me of the importance of understanding. A man came in my dad's feed and grain store and asked me if I was a Christian. I said I thought so. He looked at me hard and began to explain what he meant when he said Christian, and I realized I didn't understand. I had always prayed and gone to church because my parents taught me to do it. But it was only when I understood what it meant to have the Spirit of God living in me, giving me the power to live for him, that my prayer life became real. Since then, my prayer life has come alive. And since becoming a pastor I realize that understanding my prayer life is not only important to me but to the people I lead. If they can see me pray, and talk to me about prayer, then there's a better chance it will become important in their lives, too."

The fact that we even have to ask the question of what

drives us to prayer is, perhaps, symptomatic of our times. In biblical times, extreme circumstances drove people to their knees more often than they do today, not because we have fewer extremes today, but because we are too arrogant (or ignorant) to recognize our helplessness in the face of them. King David took his burden of leadership responsibility seriously. But he recognized his inadequacy to deal with that responsibility alone. His psalms are the result of a leader's breaking heart over his need for God's guidance and power.

In our defense, we might say that David lived in a time when the mystery of supernatural help was more easily accepted. The dangers the people of that time faced were more physical; the threat of famine and war were constant, and appealing to God (or gods) was an accepted way of handling the problems.

Today, the threats we face are more psychological than physical. Hunger does not threaten us as much as faceless anxiety. To combat anxiety, we look for solutions in counselors' offices rather than God's grace. One Christian leader said, "The problem today is that we understand everything. The knowledge explosion makes prayer anticlimactic. Researchers say that every mystery science solves opens the door to exploring even more profound mysteries. But to the man on the street, the mysteries are all solved or soon will be. Solved mysteries destroy the soil in which prayer grows best. Prayer thrives on mystery. It works best when our knowledge of God is based solely on faith."

To be sure, cultural conditions do not change the motivations to prayer. But conditions do change the form those motivations take. They also threaten us with disguising our impure motivations as pure. Indeed, it is easy to bring God requests we consider legitimate when they really are thinly disguised sin. The Scriptures teach that even prayer, the language of the Christian heart, can become misguided in subtle ways if not constantly checked against God's commands.

One particularly interesting example was Jephthah, a great warrior of Gilead. As Jephthah prepared the army for one important battle, he prayed a vow that if victory was given to Israel, he would, upon returning home in peace, sacrifice as a burnt offering to the Lord the first thing coming out of his house to meet him.

God gave Jephthah's army victory, but as he returned home, who should run out of his house to greet him? His daughter, his only child. When he saw her he tore his clothes in anguish.

Jephthah's prayer vow is an example of conjuration, an attempt to make a pact with gods and divinities, sometimes devils and other evil spirits. Such prayers arise out of a mistaken impression of what God expects of petitions. God cannot be manipulated into giving gifts. Answers to prayer are grace gifts, not forced responses.

Today we can fall into the same trap. We may not attempt to manipulate God so overtly, perhaps only because we do not recognize God's activity as widely as biblical characters did. But often our prayers for healing, to make this business deal successful, to improve our public speaking (all of which can be legitimate requests), are offered with a "deal" in mind: our faithfulness and service in return for God's positive answer. We forget to seek God's will in the matter.

Other prayers are nothing more than incantations, wishes sent to an unknown god or magic divinity. These prayers come from lack of maturity, from imperfect or nonexistent faith. These kinds of prayers can subtly sneak into our repertoire because of the culture in which we live. A prosperous culture, for example, can set living standards so high that we become consumed with goals of wealth and power. The American dream teaches that wealth is within the grasp of us all. Why should not God grant it to us? Thus it can falsely motivate our prayer under the guise of petition. To protect ourselves against impure motives, we need to understand pure ones.

Pure Motives

There are many good motivations to examine. Listen to the voices of Christian history for a sample:

Humility: "The best disposition for praying is that of being desolate, forsaken, stripped of everything" (Augustine).[4]

Fellowship: "How am I to meet God? The first thing to do is pray" (Calvin).[5]

Power: "Do not pray for easy lives. Pray to be stronger men! Do not pray for tasks equal to your powers. Pray for powers equal to your tasks" (Phillips Brooks).[6]

Protection, needs, command: "There are three reasons one should pray: because there is a Devil, as a way of obtaining things, and because it's part of the pattern God established for Christians" (R. A. Torrey).[7]

We could list many more. Motivations come out of the psychological, physiological, and sociological drives that define our humanity. They may change in intensity, scope, or focus as the conditions of our lives change. But more than anything else, they determine what we say to God and how intensely we say it.

Four motivations to prayer are widely considered fundamental to a good prayer life: Love for God, confession of sin, thanksgiving for blessings, and requests for favors. Each of these is a motivation being challenged by the modern mindset. Each, for one reason or another, is made difficult by the very fact of being a Christian leader. We will look at those challenges and difficulties in the next four chapters.

FIVE

WHEN LOVE BECOMES TRIVIAL

There is no disguise which can for long conceal love where it exists or stimulate it where it does not.

FRANÇOIS DE LA ROCHEFOUCAULD

God does not need praise by men, but he knows apriori, that when men cease to praise him, they begin to praise one another excessively.

ISAAC BASHEVIS SINGER

As I sit to write this chapter on love, I feel most unloving. Things have gone wrong all day. The weather doesn't help—it's muggy, the air heavy and oppressive, sapping my energy as the August rain drips outside. Perhaps the dreariness affected my associate. This afternoon he did something totally out of character, and I responded in kind. I got home late for supper, and my wife, not knowing when I would arrive, had nothing prepared. She offered to put slices of tomato and cheese on top of a piece of bread and grill it for me. Ugh. My stomach cringes, and all I can think about is that I have to go back to the office and write this chapter on love. Feeling as I do, how can I write about the love of God as a motivation for prayer?

None of today's incidents have made me feel unloving toward God. They make me feel unloving toward myself and toward the inconvenient incidents of life, but not toward God. My reasoning is too mundane. The muggy weather did not make me question God's providence—I know too much about meteorology for that. I did not mishandle my associate because I lacked the love of God in my heart—it was because I used an inadequate management technique. If I had phoned my wife and worked out plans for supper based on my late arrival, my stomach would not be queasy now from my pseudo-supper. I blame everything *but* God for my lack of love.

That's precisely the problem. We have so trivialized love that God is not even involved. True, the incidents of my day are simple and mundane; still, how discouraging to realize they haven't made me think of God or his love for me. Am I so indifferent? Apparently I am.

Christian leaders find several factors contribute to shove God into the background even on so central an issue as love. One is our natural inclination to be problem solvers. As anyone who has ever taken a management course realizes, the first step to solving a problem is to break it down into its constituent parts and then begin to attack each part. The problem of love, we assume, is no different.

A second, related, problem is our tendency to deal with people in the same way. Remarkable strides have been made in counseling technique the past generation. Overall, our increased expertise in becoming people helpers has been a boon to the church. But the danger (new technology always carries a danger) is the reduction of people to a conglomerate of observable behaviors.

Thus, we find ourselves not only dealing with our own love of God in a fragmented, behavioristic manner, but we tend to reinforce that approach in counseling with others. Somewhere in the process, the true nature of humanness—of love for God—gets obscured, and one of the things that suffers is our motivation to pray.

The Psychologizing of Love

We might call it the psychologizing of love. Love has come to be defined as the conglomerate of several different behaviors. This "ingredient" view of love reminds me of the report cards we received in grade school. Half of the card reported on something called citizenship. I was rated in areas like deportment, industriousness, participation, helpfulness, and clean-liness. If I scored well in all these areas, I was a good citizen of that class.

Too often we have attempted to do the same thing with love. We've taken a listing of loving behaviors, such as the one found in 1 Corinthians 13, put check marks by the ones we have observed in ourselves, and resolved to work on the ones we find missing. The problem is, love is both larger and more simple than such a list.

First, it is larger. Perhaps all the behaviors in such a list truly are the fruits of love. Still, in the case of love, the whole is larger than the sum of the parts. There is a reality to love deeper than such analysis can provide.

Second, love is also simpler. Reduced to its essence, love is a total orientation of one's being to the object of desire. Whether that object is a person, god, race, or ideal, love demands we prioritize the rest of life to meet whatever demands that object requires. Behaviors are important and can be improved or developed. But if they are divorced from a central object of desire, they lose their meaning. Christian behavior is only important if related to faith in Christ.

No group of people is more susceptible to the negative effects of reducing love to a set of behaviors more clearly than Christian leaders who deal with Christians daily, often at the crisis points of their lives. For pastors, the desire to help people is particularly strong. And what better place to start than with their overt behavior? The subtle temptation is to begin to reduce problems to observable behavior, which can be effective—until it begins to obscure the whole person's stance before God.

Judy Morford, an associate pastor at Cedar Mill Bible Church in Cedar Mill, Oregon, finds this a particular danger for those who do a lot of counseling. Judy, who does counsel-ing at Cedar Mill, says that dealing with people problems so much has convinced her people need to be dealt with as more than the sum of their behaviors:

"We have tended to psychologize everything. For example,

if someone has *some* schizophrenic behaviors, they may be labeled schizophrenic. Psychological tests designed to spot abnormalities may indicate schizophrenia. But as I talk to the people, I discover they are functioning in the mainstream of society, apparently not needing to be institutionalized. They do have some abnormal behavior patterns, but something prevents those patterns from dominating their lives. Often, after probing, I'll find it's their faith that's holding them together—praying Christians able to function in spite of their problems.

"When a high school youth gets in trouble for drinking, the tendency is to brand that youth a drinker and troublemaker, when his behavior may be prompted by a very specific thing—an argument with a close friend, for example. Psychological categorizing has made us go to two extremes: identifying people as behaviors on the one hand, and making people unresponsible for their behaviors on the other. The truth lies somewhere in the middle. Or to put it another way, without recognizing the reality of sin and God's dealing with it, you can't properly understand human beings.

"Pop psychology has affected the way we treat one another. People use terms nowadays that only psychologists used five years ago. *Self-esteem, neurotic, anxiety,* and many other words are all used now by the general population. The danger for Christians is that what we once viewed as spiritual problems are now being categorized as psychological problems, and that can lead to a cheapening of our relationship with God."

Psychologists need to define schizophrenia by lists of observable behaviors. And perhaps a *psychological* definition of love needs to be established the same way. But a *biblical* definition of love does not lend itself to such dissection, and for precisely that reason spiritual categories can never be subsumed under the psychological. Reduced to the simplest terms, psychology looks manward and spirituality looks Godward. Psychology is a good and valuable resource, but when it replaces our spirituality, we have confused our priorities.

One pastor has a sign on his desk that says simply, "Pray first." Too often we ignore that sound advice and instead analyze first.

This method of dealing with other people also affects the way we deal with ourselves. Often we think more about how we stand with other men than with God. It's something our success-oriented culture encourages. A study done not too long ago identified the eleven most common patterns of irrational thinking modern men and women exhibit. Perfectionistic self-love was at the core of most of them. For example, three of the patterns were:

• It is a dire necessity for me to be loved or approved by every significant person in my social sphere.

• I must be thoroughly competent, adequate, and achieving in all possible respects if I am to consider myself worthwhile.

• There is a perfect solution to human problems, and it is catastrophic if this correct solution is not found.[1]

Each of these problems looks for its solution in the self. At the heart is the idea that man should be able to do what only God is capable of doing. The problems we try to resolve in our modern minds are not those between God and man, but between man and man—how do I stack up against others? And if I stack up poorly, how can I improve myself to do better? Is it any wonder we have trouble loving God when we are so occupied with perfecting ourselves?

The essence of prayer is love. The biblical heroes of the faith realized that. They all begin their prayers with worship. Unfortunately, we have lost the priority of love in our prayers. Too often the prayers of modern men and women start with apology. We gratuitously pay God homage by apologizing for our imperfections, which will surely get better as soon as we get a chance to attend to the problem. "Just bear with me, God."

The result is that, for many, the Bible has ceased to be a book of choice—love God or love him not. It has become a behavioral reference book. We search its pages for clues to the proper set of behaviors that will make us lovers of God. When we find them—and the models are there—we resolve to put them into practice thereby manufacturing the "love of God" that is the primary motivation to prayer. Unfortunately, we fall short of what love really is. We end up with a kindergartener's copy of the *Mona Lisa*. And our motivation for prayer gets off on the wrong foot. In fact, it doesn't even stand up at all.

Ennobling Prayer

What can we do about restoring love to its proper place in the life of prayer? The first thing, perhaps, is simply to realize that true prayer reflects love of God, not fear of our own mortality in the face of a wrathful deity. Thomas Aquinas noted long ago, "If prayer were a cringing, whining, coaxing of a whimsical God, it would debase a man; . . . it is, in fact, the ennobling thing that has so set apart the saints from the cowardly braggarts who deify themselves and the whining cowards who dehumanize themselves."[2] Love of God, reflected in our prayers, makes us fully human.

The paradox of loving God is this: If we forget about perfecting ourselves and love our Creator, we become perfect in God. If we do it the other way around, we not only fail at perfection, but we send God a counterfeit love that further estranges us from him.[3]

Thus, we need to establish what Judy Morford calls a "first love" relationship: "I like to use the phrase, 'warp and woof' to describe the Christian's relationship to God—even though it is a cliché. The phrase comes from the weaving process, and describes the interchange of threads that make a fabric. It also applies to the Christian life. The threads must come together in a fundamental pattern, or they remain useless threads. To become cloth, they must be put together in a special way. Love of God is that fundamental pattern in the Christian's life. Without that, the threads of our life remain isolated behaviors that have no meaning, and no amount of improving the threads will make it a piece of cloth."

In teaching this to people at the church or to counselees, Morford uses the first chapter of 1 Thessalonians "where Paul presents a trilogy of things he's thankful for in the young Christians: their labor of love, their work of faith, and their hope grounded in Christ. I think it's clear that love is the basis of their work. Without it, their works are meaningless.

"My own prayer life has been through many changes over the years. As a young mother, I had a five-year-old, a three-year-old, and a one-year-old, and I found the only time I could really pray was literally in the middle of the night. If I woke up then, I would pray. As the kids grew older, I began to get up at 4:30 in the morning to pray. I still don't have ideal conditions for regular prayer. As a mother of three teenagers and working full time, I sometimes get too tired to pray. But most days I'm able to work in some time for quiet prayer.

"Because of my changing schedule over the years, I've asked myself, *Just what does God expect of me in my prayer life?* The answer I come up with is he wants a love relationship. He doesn't want a hired servant; he wants a bride. A true love will always find a way. It may not always be the same way, or the prescribed way, but it will be a way that reflects love. That's what God wants from me."

Modeling Love to One Another

Besides recognizing that prayer is grounded on a love relationship with God, we must also look to the one element of society that can still model Christian love properly—the body of Christ, the church. Joseph Sittler has observed, "Love is the function of faith horizontally just as prayer is the function of faith vertically."[4] Perhaps we must concede that we will not find much Christian love modeled in our secular society. But the church is set up to do precisely that. Both the holy catholic church and the besteepled clapboard church on the corner are living witnesses to and training grounds for what loving one another really means.

What happens when members of the body of Christ model this love to one another, both in relationships and prayer? God's will is experienced and enjoyed—and we rejoice in it together, no matter what the particular event is. It may be healing; it may be tragedy.

One pastor told two stories of love in action. One was of a young man in the congregation named Rick who had a motorcycle accident and was given almost no chance of living by the doctors attending him. If he did live, the doctors told his parents, he would be severely paralyzed. The church came out every night for a week to pray. Slowly the young man recovered and now, seven years later, is totally healed and active. The congregation rejoiced in answered prayer.

The other was a bittersweet experience. A twenty-nine-year-old mother of a two-year-old son died from cancer. "We prayed over Susan with the elders, anointing her with oil. The congregation prayed for her fervently, as we had for Rick five years earlier. But healing didn't come. In that process of frequently lifting her up to God, I learned that even when God doesn't give us what we want, he gives us the encouragement we need to go through the experience. We wanted her healed so badly, but we gave her up to God. And it became clear, even in the way she died, that God was at work.

"In both instances I saw a tremendous uniting of our body. In the first, a uniting of enthusiasm, excitement, and joy. In the second, a uniting in hurt and sorrow. A deep love for each other and God came out of both experiences, I think largely because we prayed desperately in both, but were willing to put our love for God and a desire for his will first."

What the world needs desperately is Christian love. But the world cannot manufacture it. It must come from the Source, reflected through the lovers of the Source.

SIX

SELF-REALIZATION VERSUS CONFESSION

Prayer abases intellect and pride, crucifies vainglory, and signs our spiritual bankruptcy, and all these are hard for flesh and blood to bear.

E. M. BOUNDS

Possibly, much of the flimsy piety of the present day arises from the ease with which men attain to peace and joy in these evangelistic days. We would not judge modern converts, but we certainly prefer that form of spiritual exercise which leads the soul by the way of Weeping-cross, and makes it see its blackness before assuring it that it is "clean every whit."

CHARLES HADDON SPURGEON

Before we can pray, we must be aware of our shortcomings. We must confess our sins, and confession requires humility.

Unfortunately, the church leadership role sometimes works against humility—despite the fact that the ministry is made up of tasks that must be done humbly. For example, the importance of delivering God's message to spiritually starved people three or four times a week should humble all but the most arrogant of ministers.

Yet effective preaching requires skill. The skill must be developed, and as a preacher's fluency grows, so will satisfaction with the progress. There's the problem. Spiritual work becomes secular work the minute it is tainted with pride. If the Christian leader preaches, prays, and counsels with faithfulness and even a little skill, he is praised, and the line between legitimate satisfaction and pride is threatened.

Take the counseling experience of Jim Danhof, pastor of First Covenant Church, Cedar Rapids, Iowa:

"My second year of ministry, I was in a loving, open, warm church. One of the things that goes with ministry in that kind of church is a great deal of counseling. I had some counseling abilities and some early successes. I started to think I was God's gift to the counseling universe.

"I fully enjoyed the role of messiah. But it took a great deal of time. After a year or so I was working ninety-hour weeks, and I began to realize I didn't have answers for everyone. I ran up against some walls. That summer I was dealing with three insurmountable counseling problems—the go-home-and-cry-with-your-wife type problems.

"We were coming up on vacation. I was shot. I knew I needed that vacation. My family needed the vacation. Yet here were three crises hanging fire.

"I decided I had to stay and help these families. It was my duty. I told my wife. She got angry and said, 'We're going on vacation no matter what.' I knew she was right, because I had already canceled another vacation during the year. So I said, 'All we can do is pray about the problems.' But I'm not sure I thought there was much chance it would help.

"We took our vacation. We prayed every day for those situations. I came back after two weeks expecting the worst—and all three of the problems had been solved. Completely taken care of. Without me.

"I had been struggling to get these people to understand and to work on some things, and nothing had worked. It had gotten to the place where I didn't know what to tell them. And now I come back from vacation, and none of them needed any more of my counseling.

"At that point I realized what I had been doing. I realized I don't have the healing power—God does. God could get along very well without Jim Danhof. That was a watershed experience in humility for me."

From that kind of humility about one's importance as a counselor, it is a relatively easy step to an overall recognition of one's standing before God's righteousness. None of us can measure up. That understanding is the necessary starting point of prayer. It leads to confession, and confession frees love to operate in our lives. If love is the pattern without which the cloth of prayer cannot be woven, confession is the factory whistle that signals when the weaving may begin. Nothing happens until confession takes place.

Most Christian leaders, of course, make sincere attempts at confession. The problem arises not so much in the doing of it, but in the subtle, subconscious ways confession's true intent can be subverted.

Even biblical characters struggled with honest confession. The biggest temptation for them was to regard confession as a sacrifice to appease God. This was a natural assumption given the sacrificial system Old Testament believers operated under. A fatted lamb on the altar covered all sins. If misunderstood, that could easily become a ritualistic sacrifice to appease God: *Confess guilt? Why, when all we have to do is sacrifice another lamb?* But, of course, purity of heart was still the telling test. The sacrifice was a public *form* of confession, but it was worthless without a contrite heart.

The form changed in the New Testament. Christ became the once-for-all sacrifice. Tertullian, a church father whose theological method often was to show how Old Testament practices were remade in the New Testament in light of Christ, argues that prayer in the New Testament takes the place of sacrifice in the Old Testament. In prayer, says Tertullian, we sacrifice our self-will instead of a "holocaust of rams . . . or the blood of bulls and goats" (Isa. 1:11).[1] That confession of our own spiritual bankruptcy opens the door to our petitions for mercy and succor, just as blood sacrifices opened the way to God in the Old Testament.

Today, prayer remains the chief form of our confession. But the threats to confessional prayer have changed somewhat. No longer are we teased with appeasement-related images of the altar. Now we are titillated with the self-realization gospel of the television set and movie theater. Halvor Ness, a retired pastor from Seattle, Washington, notes:

"The biggest problem with our desire to pray is the quest for self-realization, and television is the biggest offender. It preaches self-realization, and a steady diet of that is like pouring ice water inside yourself. You become cold to the claims of the gospel, and you begin looking inward instead of upward. We need to be listening to the gospel, we need preachers who preach with tears."

An Old Testament Example

One of the most instructive stories of a leader who catches himself in sin and confesses with tears is found in 2 Samuel 24. King David, chief of saints, chief of sinners, found himself leading without humility. He had taken a national census—on the surface, a harmless enough thing. But God saw David act out of kingly pride. Immediately after doing it, David realized his error. He went to the Lord and said, "What I did was very wrong. Please forgive this foolish wickedness of mine."

The Lord, through the prophet Gad, offered David three choices of punishment: seven years of famine, three days of plague, or three months of fleeing before David's enemies. David, saying it was better to fall into the hands of the Lord than those of Israel's enemies, chose the three days of plague. Seventy thousand Israelites died before God lifted the plague.

David's action and God's response are particularly instructive because the sin was not one of action, like David's adultery with Bathsheba or murder of Uriah, but one of attitude. It was a subtle case of pride. Because of its privacy, the lessons we learn about confession are all the more instructive for leaders who often find themselves making decisions in the isolation of leadership. Three lessons stand out:

First, true confession does not necessarily come about because circumstances demand it. Taking a national census was not a crime against humanity. No one was threatened by it. A census could be a good thing under certain circumstances. External pressure did not force David to confess this "sin," even though his chief military leader, Joab, suggested it was arrogant. David was king and could act contrary to his counselor's advice if he wished. He confessed because his conscience bothered him—he knew he had acted out of pride.

Second, confession must be a sincere conviction of sin. It is not public apology or ritualistic appeasement. David gained no "political" advantage because of his confession. In fact, the country suffered because he confessed. A census probably seemed a normal thing to do. The public demanded no apology; David had nothing material to gain for his confession.

Third, confession is not the end of the story. Far from it. In the short run, confession made things tougher. We don't know what would have happened to David had he not confessed his act to God. But it is hard to imagine consequences any worse than what ended up happening. Seventy thousand dead from plague—a high price to pay for sin and reconciling with God.

Why did God punish David's sin so severely? Perhaps he did not want confession confused with appeasement—confession does not mean we're off the hook. Confession does not make things easier for us. Confession does not make God look the other way about our sin. Confession does not absolve us of our responsibility. Confession prepares us for conversation with God and acceptance of his forgiveness, his terms, his sovereignty.

The Modern Problem

The danger today is not so much in confusing confession with appeasement (we hardly remember God at all, let alone a need to appease him); our danger is in viewing prayer as a means to mental health. Our results-oriented society evaluates prayer this way:

- unless it produces measurable fruits, it's ineffective.
- unless it has value to us personally, it's valueless.
- unless it outperforms TM, counseling, personal growth, and home education, what good is it?

This modern mindset predisposes us to look at prayer as a practical tool for our own benefit. Frankly, however, this "can do" spirit does not mesh well with the humility necessary for prayer.

Only one step further and the Christian leader begins to apply that pragmatic spirit to ministry and make prayer the magic wand that produces good fruit in the local church or religious organization. To be sure, it is almost always done subconsciously. But isn't that attitude the root of the lament, "I've worked so hard at this ministry; why doesn't God make me feel better about it?"

An even greater danger awaits the successful ministry, which is a greater threat to the prayer of confession than a failing ministry. H. B. London, pastor of the First Church of the Nazarene in Salem, Oregon, says, "It's hardest for me to pray properly when I am self-righteous. The moment I find myself good enough or adequate, I think I've got it made. When things are going well, it's easy for me to put prayer in the category of just one more successful program."

Prayer can be cathartic. Prayer can relax us. Prayer can make life more rewarding and fulfilling. A recently released paperback "proved" prayer was a good thing because scientific studies have shown it to do all these things. It can resolve conflict, get rid of guilt, and overcome negative complexes.

But there are days when prayer does not do any of those things. There are days when unresolved sin blocks the positive effects of prayer. It takes time to work through these things with God, and on those days, the positive psychological effects of prayer may be lacking. If we have come to view prayer as nothing more than a psyche-boosting (or church-building) technique, we are bound to be disappointed. Transcendental meditation probably has a better track record when it comes to simply making one "feel good."

One pastor confessed, "Some days prayer isn't joyous. When it isn't, I repent because I believe we're commanded to rejoice in the Lord always. We ought to feel guilty when we're not happy in God. But sometimes we aren't. And if you think of prayer as just a time to feel good, chances are you will run away from God."

We must recognize the bankrupty of thinking of prayer as the way to feel good, to be guilt-free. That is an impossible, inappropriate goal. In many ways, guilt is the surest proof of God. Guilt is not the weight of an imperfect upbringing, a decadent society, a mind twisted by legalistic parents. Guilt is God calling us back to prayer so he can tell us the reason we were created. Danish philosopher Sören Kierkegaard said, "A man could not have anything upon his conscience if God did not exist, for the relationship between the individual and God, the God-relationship, is the conscience, and that is why it is so terrible to have even the least thing upon one's conscience, because one is immediately conscious of the infinite weight of God."[2]

The prayer of confession lightens, then finally removes that weight and breaks ground for us to sow our seeds of request and petition.

SEVEN

THANKSGIVING IN A THANKLESS WORLD

Cartoon in Punch *of a man praying at bedside saying: "Is there some way you could help me, but make it look like I did it all myself?"*

Note in the "Personals" section of the Chicago Tribune: *"Thanks to God and Jesus Christ for prayers answered. K.W.G."*

Prayer of the Selfish Child
Now I lay me down to sleep,
I pray the Lord my soul to keep,
And if I die before I wake,
I pray the Lord my toys to break
So none of the other kids can use 'em . . .
Amen.

SHEL SILVERSTEIN

An old man wistfully reads the Hebrew Scripture's promise of a Messiah to come. Night after night he reads until the light or his energy wanes. Each night he prays, *O, that I could see the Messiah before I die!*

Silence is his only answer. Still he prays.

Then one night he prays and, instead of silence, God answers: *I have heard your prayer. You shall see the Promised One.*

Not sure he has heard correctly, the old man continues his yearning prayer on the nights that follow—yet the answer grows stronger, more firm. *You shall see him. You shall hold him and touch the Messiah.*

Simeon's joy was great. He was probably already an old man when God told him he would not die until he had seen the Messiah. The promised coming of the Savior was ancient, and few really believed it any more. For a man of Simeon's age, it was too much to hope for. Yet God said it would happen—and the promised day did come.

In the temple Simeon took the baby Jesus in his arms and said, "Sovereign Lord, as you have promised, you now dismiss your servant in peace. For my eyes have seen your salvation, which you have prepared in the sight of all people."

Simeon's experience in the second chapter of Luke is the paradigm of true thanksgiving. What better reason for giving thanks to God than the fact that we have all been given the chance to see the Savior? We have not held the baby Jesus in our arms, but we have been given the joy of holding him in our minds and hearts. If every other facet of our lives were negative—if we were poor, homeless, and friendless—we would still have this reason to be thankful: the fact of Jesus Christ.

Our human nature being what it is, however, very often we find the fact of Jesus Christ is not enough to help us maintain an attitude of thanksgiving. Gratitude is one of the most difficult emotions to express and maintain.

Perhaps our culture is partly to blame. Gratitude is particularly hard when everything comes easily, when our relative wealth makes us think we can, by birthright or the sweat of our brow, get whatever we need. Why should we be thankful when we've earned it on our own?

For Christian leaders, the problem is even more complex. Leaders are victim to all the gratitude-limiting pressures of a wealthy society, but as helping professionals they also suffer the ingratitude of those they serve, both lay workers and fellow leaders. Christian leaders are assailed from two directions: a sated society and a sometimes thankless Christian community.

The Problem of Wealth

Wealth is not a worldwide phenomenon. Other cultures have to still struggle to earn their daily bread, to keep their families warm and safe. Westerners who live in those cultures for even a short time discover new meaning to the word gratitude. Missionaries are typical.

Franklin and Phileda Nelson went to Burma as missionaries in the 1940s. They served there eight and a half years before the government closed the country to further missionary work. They returned to the United States where Franklin served several churches in various pastoral roles.

While in Burma they worked among remote tribes, and Franklin found his sense of gratitude for God's providence rekindled:

"In the Burmese hill country, the only way to get to remote villages was by 'shank mare.' (That's walking, in case you've never heard the phrase.) It was not at all uncommon for me to walk twenty miles a day in the dry season. When I got back to the States and worked as a pastor and church leader, I rarely walked a mile a day; the telephone and car made walking unnecessary.

"In Burma, if one of us got sick, the nearest hospital was ten days away. In the States, medical care is minutes away.

"In Burma, we'd go months without bread. Once we asked our daughter Karen to say grace before a meal, and she said, 'Why do I have to pray for my daily bread when I don't ever get any?' I have often coveted that experience for our youngest daughter who never had to wonder where her food came from. It's hard to have that sense of helplessness and humility so vital to prayer when you sit down to your daily bread and don't even think about how you got it.

"I don't in any way blame people here for not knowing what God can do. We're victims of our prosperity. But I sometimes wish we had a few more hard times so people could experience first hand how wonderful it is to be totally dependent on God."

The Problem of Thankless Followers

One denominational official lamented that for him one of the hardest things about leadership has been developing lay and professional leaders in churches, only to have them quickly forget "from whence cometh their help" and turn their backs on their benefactors as soon as they begin to make it on their own.

I asked my father, who recently retired after thirty-five years of teaching at a Christian college, if he had any regrets about his fruitful professorial career.

"I guess it would have to be the lack of gratitude by students," he said. "I never had very high expectations about students thanking me. They are in school at a difficult age—late teens and early twenties. Their identity crisis makes it a hard time psychologically for expressing thankfulness. But I did notice a steady decline over the years in what gratitude there was. It was almost as if students were never taught to be thankful. And even though I didn't expect much gratitude, I missed it all the same."

Gratitude is one of those curious emotions that grows or shrivels in direct proportion to the amount we receive from others. Pastors, especially, seem to get caught in the middle of a two-flank attack: our wealthy society discourages it, and the nature of the pastoral task often seems hopeless, helpless, and thankless. Over the past generation or two, a subtle devaluation of the pastoral role has occurred that rivals the devaluation of the dollar. In the same span that has seen the dollar shrink in buying power by almost half, the role of the pastor in the local community has probably shrunk even further. The natural respect once shown is a thing of the past. The gratitude that goes with respect is even less.

Interestingly, you don't find many pastors publicly bemoaning their reduced status. But in terms of their functioning in the community, in terms of their spiritual lives, the danger is that cynicism about the task can subtly creep in and rot the roots of thankfulness.

Gratitude Based on God Not Man

What's the solution? Perhaps to focus on the natural opportunities of Christian leadership, not its shortcomings. The call to ministry is not strictly parallel to other professional career paths. God guides his chosen leaders in profound ways. We sometimes feel frustrated with our inability to discern God's will for our lives. The factor most often overlooked in such cases is that gratitude for guidance is actually one of the things that increases its intensity. Recognition that God has directed in the past is what increases the volume of his voice in the future.

Some helpful insights for gratitude can be found in the twenty-sixth chapter of Deuteronomy. This passage outlines three elements to thanksgiving:

The first is a *concrete expression of thanks*. "Take some of the firstfruits of all that you produce from the soil of the land . . . and set it down in front of the altar of the Lord your God" (vv. 2-4). God says that when the Israelites arrive in the land and have conquered it and are living there, they must present to the Lord the firstfruits from each annual harvest. They are to take it in a basket and hand it to the priest at the temple.

It is almost paradoxical but still true today: giving increases gratitude. Psychologists tell us that the human mind grasps the concrete far more easily than the abstract. By giving a concrete expression of thanks, the abstract reality (our feeling of gratitude), the crucial part, becomes more real to us.

Sometimes the concrete gift is prayer itself. Gib Martin, pastor of Trinity Church in Burien, Washington, said, "Bonhoeffer wrote that the Psalms were God's gift to the church, and when we have nothing else to give God, we can give those back to him in the form of prayers. I have tried that and reaped the benefits."

The second element is to *remember difficulties God has seen you through*. Verses five to nine say that after the priest has accepted the gifts in the name of God, the people should recite a brief history of their being freed from Egypt and given a new fertile land. In this illustration, the children of Israel remember what it was like to live in Egypt. For us it is the remembrance or recognition of what we are like without God. After all, that is the crucial factor. What is it like not to hold the Messiah in our hearts and minds? Bleak, desolate, hopeless.

One Christian leader said she uses the harder times of her life to combat current crises: "I'm a person who is always ready with plan B or C if plan A doesn't work out. I think my experiences have forced me to develop that attitude. I once had three major surgeries in three months. I had no control over what would happen with my life then. Remembering those brick walls helps me understand God's sovereignty and the potter/clay relationship."

Perhaps for today's Christian leaders, fellowship needs are greater than any other. Most local churches, for example, are one-person pastorates, and most are operated in entrepreneurial fashion. Fellowship languishes under such conditions. No camaraderie with staff, no employer to unload on, no evaluation sessions to tell you how it's going. Ministerial associations usually turn into brag sessions rather than brainstorming sessions. The minister feels cut off from the warmth of peer support.

Again, Franklin Nelson's experience on the mission field is instructive. "Like the pastorate in the States, the mission field can be lonely. I remember when our first daughter was born. Several days after her birth I had to visit some villages. It would take two weeks. After a couple days out I began to feel sorry for myself. I was alone, climbing steep hills, no one to talk to and tell about my new daughter.

"I asked the Lord for some sign that he was with me. I didn't know what I wanted him to do because I didn't know what would help me. As far as I knew, it was impossible to cheer me up. But I asked God to do it anyway.

"The middle of that afternoon I came to a village. It was a new Christian village that was just beginning to get grounded spiritually, so I didn't expect the warm welcome of old friends. But to my surprise, they came out en masse singing a welcome song. I hadn't planned on spending the night there, but they asked me to. They took me to a hut they had cleaned up very nicely. I decided to stay.

"This overwhelming hospitality and love, totally unexpected, answered my prayer. It was simple, something we expect almost as a matter of course back home. But it was just what I needed at that time."

Remembrances of God's love in good times and bad can stimulate our gratitude.

The third element is *to be grateful for what the Lord has made out of us*. After reciting the litany of our once-lost-now-found status, the Lord says to "rejoice in all the good things the Lord your God has given to you and your household" (v. 11). Like Simeon who held the baby Jesus and rejoiced, we should be ever aware that God has worked, is working, and will continue to work in our lives.

For Christian leaders, then, the key to developing a deep thankfulness is to not base our gratitude on the uncertain status of wealth and prosperity, nor the fickle gratitude of those we serve. The Christian leader's gratitude must be based on a deep satisfaction in ministries faithful to God's will.

Gordon Johnson is a semi-retired pastor of College Avenue Baptist Church in San Diego. Before coming to California, Gordon had been dean of a Christian college and had held several pastorates.

"Gratitude for me comes only when I focus strictly on what God has done in my life. For example, I pray for guidance more often than anything—and God has always answered.

"When I was serving a church in Chicago, I had two job offers at once. One was to become dean of students at a Christian college. They asked first, and after interviewing there, I was pretty convinced I would go if the college trustee board approved the call. I went back to Chicago and preached in my church on Sunday morning. After the service representatives from another church in the area came up and asked if they could take me and my family out to dinner. We had no other commitments, so I agreed. At dinner they asked me if I would come to pastor their church. I was thrown into a terrible confusion. *Why is God doing this? What is he trying to tell me?*

"That week an official letter of invitation came from both the church and the college. I prayed about both at length and finally wrote a letter of acceptance to the college and a letter of rejection to the other church. My wife typed the letters, and I remember sitting on the edge of my bed that evening looking at them both. I felt sick, plagued by inner doubt. *You're just getting emotional about this,* I thought. *Get them in the mail and that will give you some peace.*

"I walked to the corner mailbox and dropped the letters in. But when I got back home, I felt sicker and sicker about the whole thing. About eleven o'clock that night I called the post office to see if I could get the letters back. 'Too late,' they said. They had already gone.

"The next morning I called the college president and asked if he would please ignore the letter he was about to receive from me. I did the same with the pastoral search committee. Then I got on a train and went back to the college for one more look. By the end of that visit I decided being dean of students wasn't for me, and I turned down their invitation. I also declined the invitation from the other church.

"Looking back, I think God used the invitation from the church to get me to rethink the way he was working in my life. He used that and my dis-ease during my prayers."

Had Gordon not asked the fundamental question of *What is God trying to tell me in this?* his prayer for guidance might have been the much more self-centered *Please God, which of these offers will be the best for me?*

If we gauge our gratitude on worldly wealth and opportunity, we may someday find ourselves in Franklin Nelson's shoes in Burma with no worldly wealth to celebrate. If we gauge gratitude on the thankfulness of those around us, human nature will disappoint us. Nine of ten healed lepers ran away without thanking even Jesus.

If, however, we gauge gratitude by the way God has worked in our lives, then nothing the world withholds can dispel our thanksgiving, and we can even rejoice in the pettiness of those around us because we can say, "Lord Jesus, thank you for the opportunity of working with these your children so obviously in need of your love." To those who seek, God provides the grace to be gracious.

EIGHT

ARTICULATING OUR REQUESTS

In the situation Western man finds himself, we can supply no demonstration of the necessity for prayer or even of its usefulness. It is futile to pretend that prayer is indispensable to man. Today he gets along very well without it.

JACQUES ELLUL

You have not because you ask not.

JAMES 4:2

God answers our prayers, and he does not seem to begrudge doing so. He displays good will and cheer—at times, an almost puckish sense of humor.

Consider Genesis 18 where Abraham learns God is going to destroy the cities of Sodom and Gomorrah. Abraham is horror stricken and pleads on behalf of Sodom: "Will you sweep away the righteous with the wicked? What if there are fifty righteous people in the city?"

The Lord answers, "If I find fifty righteous people in the city of Sodom, I will spare the whole place for their sake."

Abraham decides fifty might be a touch high: "What if the number is five less than fifty? Will you destroy the whole city because of five people?"

"If I find forty-five there, I will not destroy it."

Sensing he's on to something good, Abraham asks, "What if only forty . . .?"

The Lord agrees.

Thirty?

Again the Lord agrees.

Twenty?

Yet again the Lord agrees.

Abraham pauses, possibly weighing his chances of finding even twenty godly people in a place like Sodom, the 42nd Street of the ancient Near East. Finally he works up his courage for one last request: "May the Lord not be angry, but let me speak just once more. What if only ten can be found there?"

God is not angry, probably just bemused. After all, he knows how many godly people are in Sodom: "For the sake of ten, I will not destroy it."

With that, Abraham quits asking, and we're left wondering: Would God have agreed to spare Sodom if Abraham had asked on the basis of merely one righteous man? Perhaps. But Abraham didn't try. Was God looking for an advocate for Sodom—someone who cared? Abraham cared, but apparently not enough to risk asking God to save Sodom for the sake of one godly person.

God delights, the Bible says, in giving his people good gifts. Some Scriptures offer God's help; others command us to make prayer requests so that he can answer them. Question 129 of the Heidelberg Catechism says the answer to our prayers is more certain than our awareness of things we ask for.[1] The "problem" of unanswered prayer lies not in any reluctance on God's part, but in our inability to articulate our requests properly and then accept God's answer—whether a positive answer or negative. Two problems, in particular, prevent us from seeing our prayers answered.

We Don't Think To Ask

In many areas of our lives, we simply do not consult God. Vance Havner said that what we used to call worldliness we now call secularization. Both mean we think world first instead of God first. We live in a desacralized, lay world. The sacred dimension to life is no longer assumed, as it was in Abraham's time. God does not figure in the world's plans. He is not opposed as much as merely ignored.

The reason that secularization is so dangerous for Christian leaders is that secularization does not harm "religion" at all. A false definition of secularization would be that it is the withering of religion. But as Richard John Neuhaus has pointed out, that has not occurred. If secularization harmed organized religion, we would expect to have fewer churches. But we actually have more. We would expect the proportion of people attending church to be down. But the proportion is greater. We would expect declines in religious rites as opposed to civil alternatives (marriages and funerals), less religious income, less religious literature, and a dwindling of new sects and new movements. But in fact they have all increased. By these standards, religion is doing very well.[2]

Secularization is growing along with religion. Secularization, properly defined, is a viewpoint that becomes more and more man-centered and less and less God-centered. By that definition we begin to understand the negative impact it has had on prayer life.

A common reason given for prayerlessness is busyness. Often the busyness comes from success. One reason for organized religion's drift toward man-centeredness is the number of people involved. As churches and organized religion grow, we sense a need to get a rope around the growth—but we forget to let God tie the knot. As management science and demographic technology become more precise, we forget the role God plays in the building of his church. Pure prayer is the sincere crying out of a heart with nowhere else to turn; our fast-changing technology seemingly provides solutions to a lifetime's worth of turning points, and we are never finally forced to our knees. Our competence in matters organizational leaves no room to lose our dignity before God, the essential precondition of asking for help.

For Christian leaders, a prime illustration is the church business meeting. One pastor said, "For a long time it seemed like we couldn't integrate the secular and spiritual aspects of our business meetings. Prayer and Bible study was always something we tacked on at the beginning or the end; in between we did our business without considering the spiritual ramifications. Two and a half years ago we were at our annual board retreat and realized that we hadn't been praying regularly. So the members committed to a weekly prayer meeting at 6:30 Friday morning. They have been remarkably faithful in attending so they must think it's working. We've started to get better at making spiritual decisions at our business meetings, too. But we still have a long way to go."

C. S. Lewis in his *Letters to Malcolm: Chiefly on Prayer*, writes, "Those who do not turn to God in petty trials will have no habit or such resort to help them when the great trials come. So those who have not learned to ask him for childish things will have less readiness to ask him for the great ones. We must not be too high minded. I fancy we may sometimes be deterred from small prayers by a sense of our own dignity rather than of God's."[3]

We Don't Ask Correctly

Asking incorrectly is epidemic. One leader remembered his experience as a young air force officer in Japan "in the days when getting assigned to Vietnam was a great thing for your military career."

He said, "I pulled all the strings I could to get assigned there, and finally the papers did get through. I had also prayed God would help me move up. I would be promoted an additional rank, which meant I would be the youngest person of my rank in the entire air force. In fact, everything in my military career had gone great up to that point.

"I was planning to attend an important religious conference in the U.S. on my leave before going to Vietnam. But when my orders came through, I found they had extended me in Japan one month, and I would miss the conference. I immediately went to see the squadron commander to see if there was any way I could get out of the assignment. He said it was too late, the orders had already come through.

"My shrewd career moves forced me to miss a spiritual experience I had been looking forward to. Suddenly it struck me that I had allowed my career to overshadow God in my life. I had placed so much stock in manipulating my career that I had left out the hand of God. I went back to my barracks and fell on my knees and said, 'God, from now on my life is in your hands. No more premature pushing and pulling from me. I'll do my best, and trust you to take it from there.' That was the first time I really felt free in my prayer to God. It was because I finally realized I was too imperfect to ask for some things in my life, and that I could only pray for God's will."

Incorrect requests are often uttered, even by Christian leaders. At times, our prayer requests go unanswered because they are poorly formed or presumptuous. We do not take time to discover what the true, pure desires of our hearts should be, and thus offer up incomplete, half-hearted requests that God would be a fool to answer.[4] Just what are the gremlins that invade our psyches, causing such weak, inappropriate requests?

We are impatient. We live in a fast-paced world and want quick answers. Ole Hallesby in his classic book on prayer uses Mary the mother of Jesus as the model for the lesson of waiting on God's time and judgment. He refers to John 2:1-11, the story of the wedding festivities at Cana when the hosts run out of wine. Mary simply tells Jesus, "We have no more wine." She then waits for him to do something about it, instructing the servants to stand by and carry out Jesus' bidding.[5]

Hallesby says this is a paradigm for our requests: State our condition and wait. Too many of us suffer from prayer fatigue because we feel we have to lay out all possible solutions before God and help him make the decision. We may need to do that for ourselves, but not for God.

Several years ago my sister, a public school teacher, told me she was worrying about whether to accept a teaching contract offered by another school district or stay in her current school. Trying to help, I began asking her some fundamental questions: "What are your real options?" It turned out that neither school had actually offered her a contract yet. (This was in a period of declining enrollments, and teaching jobs were year-to-year question marks.) Her worrying was based on possibilities, not facts.

In a sense, our approach to God should be well informed. He wants us to express our problem from which we want relief as clearly and sincerely as possible. But we must ask expecting God to act, not as a rubber stamp for our agenda, but as a superior, active agent who has final control over our lives.

We forget to tie our needs into the larger needs of the body of Christ. Narcissism can only be counteracted by involvement in a group. The church can perform that function even in the case of highly individualistic needs. Many Christian leaders mention the importance of formal or informal prayer groups at the church and how that helps them keep perspective in their personal prayer lives.

Bob Dickson, pastor of Hope Presbyterian Church in Richfield, Minnesota, has a card under the clear plastic that protects his desk. It reads: "When we work, we work; when we pray, God works."

"That card," he says, "helps me do two things: (1) keep prayer at the top of my priority list and (2) keep me open to the way God works in the prayer lives of the people at our church. A couple of years ago, my wife, Gloria, got an idea for a prayer ministry here based on Ezekiel 47, the passage that talks about a river coming out of the temple, which we see as a river of prayer. As we have instituted the program, we now have over a hundred individuals on a regular basis going into our sanctuary with notebooks of prayer requests from our people. If one of our members has a problem, over a hundred people will be praying for that request.

"This program has had a tremendous impact on me as pastor. The distractions that attend a busy ministry—the phone, people, problems, meetings—are the biggest obstacles to my own prayer life. Yet I can walk across the hall to the sanctuary and in twenty minutes sense the Spirit's presence as other people there are lifting up our church's prayer needs to God. By burying my needs in with those of the entire congregation's, I gain perspective, peace, and comfort from knowing I am merely one of the body."

We evaluate answered prayer by material not spiritual standards. God may answer our prayers in a material way. He may also answer by giving us the spiritual strength to cope with a material loss—even as we have been praying that he would help us avoid the material loss. God's idea of answered prayer is much broader than ours.

Martin Buber tells the story of a man who was afflicted with a terrible disease. He complained to Rabbi Israel that his suffering interfered with his learning and praying. The rabbi put his hand on his shoulder and said: "How do you know, friend, what is more pleasing to God, your studying or your suffering?"[6]

In the end, we do not know what God wants even when we bring requests to him that seem quite obvious. It is difficult to give up the "obvious" to an unseen, spiritual Being. But that is what faith is all about. It is also a fundamental element of answered prayer.

N I N E

MAKING PRAYER A HABIT

I am therefore not really deeply worried that prayer is at present a duty, and even an irksome one. This is humiliating. It is frustrating. It is terribly time wasting. The worse one is praying the longer one's prayers take, but we are still only at school.

C. S. LEWIS

Our abandonment of one thing is not sufficient to settle us in the habitual practice of the other, but there is need again of some fresh impulse, and of an effort not less than that made in our avoidance of evil dispositions, in order to our acquiring good ones.

JOHN CHRYSOSTOM

Many problems go away if you just leave them alone. Try to fix them and you only make them worse. Most stomach aches, rainstorms, and sour moods, for example, eventually disappear if you ignore them as best you can.

Other problems go away only if you deal with them thoughtfully, thoroughly, and persistently. They need attention. Left alone they slip into the nagging subconscious, but they never go away. The problem of developing a consistent prayer life falls into this category. Without some effort, prayer will not become significant.

Let's assume, for a moment, you want to work at prayer—whether out of love for or obedience to God, you want to make prayer a regular part of your life. What now?

First we must recognize some dangers in pursuing a habit of prayer. Focusing too heavily on the mechanics of prayer can defeat the very purpose of it. Any time the mechanics of prayer get in the way of loving God, they are useless. Dry, joyless prayer results.

It is somewhat akin to the lack of joy you see in some picture takers. You've seen them. They abound at vacation spots and scenic overlooks. They are driven to photograph things even if it means discomfort and distraction to themselves and their loved ones—even if it means they miss seeing the very thing they are trying to photograph.

As a confirmed nonphotographer, I've tried to analyze this compulsion. From my sanctimonious perch, I've decided these people are trying to package their experiences for future reference even as they are happening. Instead of trusting their own senses to store and process the beautiful scenes and new experiences, they feel they must photograph them so they are stored in a "safe" place, outside their own minds.

An experience approached with blind compulsion can obscure many of its aspects. A photograph, even though perfectly composed, exposed, and developed, will never be able to retain the essence of the experience. Photographers are often left holding in their hands lots of memories but have little to remember. Unless we let our full range of emotions enrich our vision, we have lost something most important.

Focusing too heavily on the mechanics of prayer can produce a similar result. We may pray every day for an hour, and yet the product can be dry, lifeless words sent compulsively heavenward. There is an element to prayer that goes beyond definition, that depends on the mysterious working of the Holy Spirit in the lives of men and women.

A further danger, though, is that we will develop the habit of prayer mindlessly, adopting a prepackaged form without considering how it fits our unique needs. Interestingly, research has shown that habits need to be intensely individualized things. People form them in similar patterns, but the actual content of the habits themselves are unique combinations of the action and the person's personality.

Knight Dunlap, in his book *Habits*, illustrates this with a laboratory experiment. Volunteers are given some routine mathematical work to do on adding machines. As they are working, an experimenter sneaks up without warning and discharges a pistol behind them. Predictably, the reaction to this loud noise is almost always violent. But the interesting feature of the experiment is what happens when the process is repeated. Some of the subjects react much less violently, while others react even more violently. In either case, the subject is forming a "habitual" way of responding to the stimulus. But the response itself is quite individualistic and cannot be predicted.[1]

Forming a prayer habit, at regular times and places, does not mean we conform our prayer life so rigidly to someone else's pattern that we lose the spontaneity of God working in our lives. It leaves freedom, yet gives form to a lover's anxious desire for the lover. Or as Proverbs 8:34-36 (TLB) says, "Happy is the man who is so anxious to be with me that he watches for me daily at my gates, or waits for me outside my home! For whoever finds me finds life and wins approval from the Lord. But the one who misses me has injured himself irreparably. Those who refuse me show that they love death."

One young pastor said, "God is like a father who wants a relationship with his son. I can think of a lot of families that don't have a good father-son relationship. Usually it's because they don't talk—or can't because of years of poor communication. I think God feels toward me like I feel toward my two-year-old son—I can't wait until he learns to talk so I can figure out what's going on inside his head, and he can learn to love me as a friend as well as a father."

How are regular habits formed? The scientific literature on the subject almost always is prefaced with three questions:[2]

1. *Are you committed to breaking the old habit and forming a new one?* One of the most important factors in a commitment to prayer is a positive role model. Paul Rees, lecturer for World Vision, says, "I can still remember my father arising early every morning and going into his study for prayer. I knew what was going on in there, and it had an influence on my prayer life that lasts to this day. My sister-in-law is another. She's past eighty now, but has been a hard-working woman all her life. She conveys this feeling of how incredibly real the Lord is to her and how easy it is for her to listen and speak to him. I always come away from meeting with her renewed in

my resolve to make the Lord that real in me so others see him in what I do."

Christian leaders continually referred to role models of prayer. Often it was a father, mother, grandfather, or grandmother. Sometimes it was a contemporary. Occasionally it was a biblical hero. One leader mentioned the psalmist as her model: "Psalm 61 recognizes the need for making a commitment to pray, and versus 5-8 have always been an encouragement to my prayer life: 'For you have heard my vows, O God; to praise you every day, and you have given me the blessings you reserve for those who reverence your name. You will give me added years of life, as rich and full as those of many generations, all packed into one. And I shall live before the Lord forever. Oh send your lovingkindness and truth to guard and watch over me, and I will praise your name continually, fulfilling my vow of praising you each day.' "

2. *Are you in control of your life to make the changes necessary?* When people feel they can control some conditions, success is more likely. One study showed that when students were given a choice in selecting the classes they took, they performed significantly better on exams and reported greater satisfaction with their classes and instructors than did students who had no choice.[3] Another study showed that when opportunities were available to choose between several alternative ways of doing a complex task, performance improved.[4] Rigid insistence that filing, for example, be done in one particular way gave less satisfaction to most secretaries than when they were given an opportunity to work out their own procedures within broad company guidelines.

The implications for prayer are obvious. In order to give yourself the best chance to develop the habit, you need to feel you can control yourself and the form the prayer habit takes. Considering the variety of successful prayer practice we see in those around us, this should be possible if a person is willing to look for the alternatives.

Bill Bump, pastor of the Free Methodist Church of Wheaton, Illinois, said, "The most difficult thing about prayer for me was thinking I had to use someone else's method and match their expectations. Then I discovered that I work best using short periods of intense concentration; so I matched my prayer practice to that strength by having many short prayer times throughout the day. Once I realized this kind of prayer was all right with God, I found my guilt gone and my prayer much more intense."

3. *Are you willing to make the changes necessary?* Willingness to act is the final step. Resolve and opportunity do not mean much if action doesn't follow. If action doesn't follow the other two steps, then guilt will result. The psychological principle of evaluative consistency says that we have a basic need for what we *think* about a subject to match up with what we *do* about a subject.[5]

D. Martyn Lloyd-Jones in his book, *Spiritual Depression: Its Causes and Cure*, put it a little differently. The central cause of spiritual depression, he said, "is due to the fact that you are listening to yourself instead of talking to yourself." The right way to do it, he says, is as the psalmist does in Psalm 42 when he says, "Why art thou cast down, O my soul? Why art thou disquieted within me?"[6] At some point we must take hold of ourselves and act.

Steps Toward a Habit of Prayer

Are there steps we can take to form the habit of prayer? Stanton Peele, a social psychologist who has been investigating the problem of addiction for over a decade, has concentrated his study on what is required to break a bad habit and start a new one. Most of his work has been done with reformed alcoholics and drug abusers.[7]

In studying the pattern of these recoveries, Peele has identified four distinct stages. Although his research has been done with extreme cases, the stages seem to apply broadly.

The first stage is recognizing that the life we are now living is not the life we want to live. We finally, through accumulated unhappiness and recognition of our fallen state, realize that we want to do better. In terms of prayer, it would mean finally recognizing the futility of trying to make it without prayer.

The second stage is a flash of insight, a moment of truth when a decision to change is made. It's the kind of experience Paul had on the Damascus Road. Life takes a 180-degree turn. In a moment of decision an alcoholic vows never to take another drink, a smoker lays down his cigarettes forever, a heroin user throws away the needle. It may not be easy, but he never looks back. It's at that point a nonpray-er suddenly decides to pray.

The third stage is putting flesh on the moment-of-truth decision by changing life patterns to accommodate the new lifestyle. For the pray-er this means ordering our environment to encourage prayer. Attend prayer meetings, read literature that encourages prayer, associate with friends who pray and will talk about it with us, make a place and time in our life for regular prayer.

The fourth stage is changing one's self-perception. No longer are we non-prayers; now we are praying persons and identify ourselves thus.

The next four chapters will look at each of these stages in more detail. We will give examples of Christian leaders who decided to become pray-ers, and we will find that they went through stages very much like the four we just described. Some of the stories resemble Damascus Road experiences. Most of them sound more mundane—they would be mundane, in fact, if they weren't stories of God working in people's lives.

TEN

I NEED TO CHANGE

The worst sin is prayerlessness. Overt sin or crime or the glaring inconsistencies which often surprise us in Christian people are the effect of this or its punishment. We are left by God for lack of seeking Him.

P. T. FORSYTH

We are not free to pray or not to pray, nor to pray only when we feel so inclined. For prayer is not an activity which is natural to us. Prayer is a grace, and we can expect this grace only from the Holy Spirit.

KARL BARTH

Before any habit can be broken or formed, we need to become convinced that change is necessary. Until then, nothing will happen. The natural inclination of our psyches is to maintain the status quo. Something needs to happen to get us off dead center.

What can move us off dead center? Often the happening is the result of an accumulated unhappiness at the way life is going.[1] Other times it's a specific incident, something we read, or a friend finally setting us straight.

Theophan the Recluse wrote at length about what it takes to incite change. Change begins "the moment your heart starts to be kindled with divine warmth. But you must realize that this kindling cannot take place in you while the passions are still strong and vigorous. Passions are the dampness in the fuel of your being, and damp wood does not burn. There is nothing else to be done except to bring in dry wood from outside and light this, allowing the flames from it to dry out the damp wood, until this in its turn is dry enough to begin slowly to catch alight."[2]

The "dry wood" brought in from the outside differs from person to person. Some of us require oak logs; others of us are warmed by birch. The following four accounts illustrate quite different ways in which the recognition of our inherent need for prayer becomes real. Perhaps you'll find yourself in one of them.

Learning Through Personal Trial

John Frey and his wife were driving on Interstate 80 across the flat plains of Nebraska. The monotony of the long drive ended in Kearney, where Frey had a heart attack.

Frey is telling the story in his sunshine-filled office at his Midwest church. At sixty-five years of age, Frey is preparing to retire after more than forty years of pastoring several Christian Reformed churches, but his full head of thick white hair and his trim build suggest a younger man, certainly not one who experienced a life-threatening heart attack just twelve months earlier.

"As I lay in the hospital bed," he says, "I saw nothing but billowing clouds of the most intense white I have ever seen. Psalm 103:2, 3 ran across my mind: 'Bless the Lord, O my soul, and forget not all his benefits. He forgives all my sins and heals all my diseases.' I had been lying there in extreme pain, but all of a sudden I got a peace that was beyond understanding. I felt clean. It was as if I was being cleansed to match the clouds I was seeing. It's a fabulous experience to know you can be on the verge of death and be calm and feel clean before a righteous God."

Frey had been airlifted from Kearney to Lincoln where doctors performed bypass heart surgery. But the story for Frey and his wife was the prayer support they received from others. Never before had prayer seemed so essential, so like food and air to their wilting spirits.

"A Baptist church in Kearney befriended my wife the days we were there. The pastor came daily to pray with me. When we got to Lincoln, a family we didn't know that lived near the hospital opened their house to my wife and daughters. God's salt is sprinkled throughout society. When you need it, it's there. That experience taught me more about prayer.

"I had long known the value of personal prayer. I attended the International Congress on Evangelism in Minneapolis in 1969, and there I learned to be open to the moving of the Holy Spirit. I found a freedom in prayer that I didn't have before. I realized God didn't want John Frey to be anyone but John Frey. I found a joy in the ministry I never had until that time.

"Those two experiences—the Congress on Evangelism and the heart attack—taught me what I know about prayer. I'm not a perfect pray-er by any means. But I never underestimate its importance. And I'm always open to learning more as God teaches."

Learning Through People's Needs

For Doug Hazen, prayer became vital when he felt a burden for the community of Eugene, Oregon: "Last February three things happened almost simultaneously that convinced me to pray for our community.

"First, we had an evangelism conference here at the church, which sensitized me to the needs of this community.

"Second, I read a study done by a University of Washington sociologist that concluded that Eugene had one of the lowest rates of church attendance of any community in the country. The study also showed there was a direct relationship between low church attendance and cult activity. That's certainly true in Eugene. We're in the top ten in cult activity and the last of the 215 communities rated in church attendance.

"Third, economic conditions here are not good. We have a couple of families in our church with small businesses who are facing bankruptcy right now.

"I did a lot of thinking about that on my daily commute. I sensed a personal need to pray for this community. I'm just one guy out of 105,000, and I realize I can't change the world in my own power. But I do have the power of the Holy Spirit to draw from, and the way to tap into that is through prayer.

"Now I find that the evangelizing of our community is a

natural occasion for prayer. In a sense, our church's mission forces me to pray. I don't pray because I have to, but because it is fundamental to loving people.

"Not long ago we had a critical board meeting. Both the senior pastor and I felt under the gun, and we spent a lot of time praying about it. God gave us the wisdom to deal with the situation, and I remember how comfortable I felt about prayer being the central point of our deliberation."

Learning Through Books

Books can teach something of life and prayer. Norris Magnuson talked about their importance to him as he sat in the special collections room of the Bethel Theological Seminary library, where he is librarian. In one corner sat F. O. Nillson's steamer trunk that came over with the first Swedish settlers. The walls are lined with large paintings of other Swedish and Norwegian faithful who led Bethel Seminary after its founding in 1871. An ancient lectern from some early Swedish Baptist church sits imposingly in one corner.

"It's possible to read about giants of spiritual history and feel challenged rather than guilty about the contrast between their lives and mine. For example, Frank Laubach. The story of his awakening is moving. And his little practical booklet, *The Game With Minutes*, on deepening one's walk with God makes the whole process fun. Yet there's never a question that it's an enormously urgent undertaking.

"I have also been challenged negatively at times by the things I've read. P. T. Forsyth, in *The Soul of Prayer*, says, 'The worst sin of all is the sin of prayerlessness.' That jarred me. Maybe prayerlessness *is* the root of all negatives. If God doesn't factor into our life in some way, we're lost. Prayer opens our lives to God and makes us functioning Christians.[3]

"In *The Struggle of Prayer*, Donald Bloesch talks about busyness being the new holiness. I find time to be my biggest problem. Time and the fact that our culture doesn't want the things that Christ wanted. Servitude, obedience, suffering, hanging on the cross—all of them run counter to our society's values.[4]

"My models of prayer have tended to be biblical and historical. That's probably why I'm an historian. Augustine, Luther, Wesley—all very gifted, learned, and earnest persons—were preeminently persons of prayer. Deep personal encounters with God freed them into their remarkable life works. Jonathan Edwards, the pietist Zinzendorf, Charles Finney, and other notable leaders were similarly marked by prayer. Working in the pietistic heritage of Swedish Baptists as well as in the larger evangelical awakenings, has increased my awareness of the central role of prayer in the Christian story. It has also made me agree with A. W. Tozer when he said, 'Listen to the one who listens to God.' "

Learning Through Ministry

Prayer is not necessarily easier for men and women in local church ministry. Pressures of being "spiritual giants" can inhibit growth. The need for the church to "make it" can turn the leader into an administrator and organizer rather than a servant concerned with the spiritual well-being of those in the flock.

Scotty Clark had just resigned as pastor of the Friends Church in Silverton, Oregon. Constant bickering with the Christian education committee about church programs and infighting with the elders had destroyed what was left of his ministerial idealism. He walked into the church's prayer chapel, raised his fist and shook it in the face of God. "If this is all there is to being a minister, then I just can't handle it." His anger vented, he slumped to his knees and prayed.

"I remember dissecting myself, giving the parts to God: 'Here's my mind, Lord, it's yours. Here are my hands, Lord, they're yours . . . I can't handle this by myself. I'm your servant.'

"It was the most moving prayer experience I have ever had. I felt like the weight of the whole church was lifted from my shoulders, and I became filled with an energy that I haven't experienced since."

For thirty days he was on a spiritual high. He slept only about three hours a night. He wrote sermons that flowed in one sitting. He prayed through the list of church families daily. "When I went into the pulpit, I felt a sense of compassion for and an identity with the people that had been totally absent before.

"One Sunday shortly after this experience, I preached a sermon on Jesus' teaching about the narrow way and the broad way. I called on the people to open themselves to the love and discipline of Christ in a fresh way. After we sang three choruses of 'I Surrender All,' eight people, including several elders, came to the front for prayer. Some of them were the ones I had been fighting with. I stepped from the platform and prayed with each one individually. Afterward they said, 'Scotty, you prayed exactly what I was feeling and thinking.' That was probably the most profound experience of discernment and positive feedback I have ever had with prayer.

"I was able to give myself to prayer and teaching the Word of God in the remaining five months of that ministry. I felt free to minister rather than trying to make the church go, and I discovered more things about true ministry than at any period of my ministry up to that point.

"Even though prayer has become a bedrock of my ministry, I'm still a babe in the woods when it comes to prayer. I'd like to have a long quiet time with the Lord every morning, but frankly I've never been able to achieve that. I pray on the run. When people telephone and ask for prayer, I pray with them right there over the wires. If someone stops me after the morning service and asks for prayer, I pull them aside and pray right there. I pray sentence prayers throughout the day as they become needed.

"I wish I could say I love to pray all the time, but there's something about this flesh that resists it. I used to think that there were universally applicable techniques to learning how to do it—that if I followed them perfectly God would be pleased and prayer would be easy. I don't believe that anymore. Now I think God calls us all to a unique style of prayer to fit us. Our task is to discover what our style is. That's what I pray God will teach me—my style."

The need to pray is unique. The way it finally bores its way into our souls and becomes a permanent feature of our lives is as unique as our conversion experience, for it is in fact a reflection of our relationship with God. Samuel Chadwick said, "Prayer is the privilege of sons and the test of sonship. It would seem as if God divides all men into the simple classification of those who pray and those who do not. It is a very simple test, but it is decisive and divisive."[5]

One Christian leader remembered his intense search for prayer as a young pastor. "I felt so strongly that I needed to pray more; I decided to spend three days alone to fast and pray. Near the end of that time I felt an urging to call a man I had confidence in as a spiritual leader. I asked him to come pray for me.

"He lived quite a distance away and so I told him to come only if it seemed right to him. He thought about it and prayed for a day, and then said he'd come. He came, and I was all ready to prostrate myself before him and let him pray over me. Yet the first thing he did was sit down in front of me and begin to confess all *his* sins. I sat there thinking, *What are you doing? I'm supposed to do that for you*. He kept doing it, though, and I remained quiet. Finally, he said, 'Now, do you still want me to pray for you?'

"Then I realized what he was trying to tell me. I had looked to him as a spiritual giant, able to tell me how to fill my need for prayer. He had the discernment to see that, and he wouldn't help me until I fully realized that it was a matter between God and me. Once he saw I understood that, we began to talk about my spiritual needs."

The need for prayer is between each person and God. He may use a friend, books, ministry, or other events to point us to that need, but those are only tools to get us face to face with God. Once there, we have a decision to make.

ELEVEN

SOMEONE TO STAND IN THE GAP

Most addicts can pinpoint a moment at which they "hatched" from the addiction and left it behind.

STANTON PEELE

Once convinced of the need for prayer, how does someone form the habit of prayer? Is it a slow gradual process? Or does commitment come quickly, like a flash of insight?

Psychologists who study habit formation say that sometimes habits are made, or broken, in moment-of-truth experiences. Stanton Peele, after studying the problem of addiction for more than a decade, says that more often than we'd expect alcoholics, for example, simply decide a life of drinking is no longer worth it, and quit. No long drawn out withdrawal, no professional help—just a sudden realization that drinking is not what they want to do anymore.[1]

Peele admits, however, that these "moments of truth" can be identified only in retrospect. They cannot easily be predicted, and they cannot be manufactured in a one-two-three-step process. They seem to be the result of several needs and factors coming together in a person's life at one point so the weight of making the decision becomes compelling. Psychologists have noted that often one need by itself is not enough to stimulate action toward a good goal, but if two or three needs are recognized that could be satisfied by the same goal, change is not only possible but likely. Is it possible that our "bad habit" of prayerlessness can be overcome by a moment of truth?

Alec Rowlands, pastor of First Assembly of God in Cedar Rapids, Iowa, had an experience like this with his prayer life. Perhaps some elements of his story will be helpful to those of us still hoping to be struck by a blinding flash of light, or at least have our darkness illumined by the light of a steadily burning candle.

Rowlands wanted revival for his church. He prayed for it. He read and reread the first fifteen chapters of Acts, searching for clues to the first-century church's secret of Spirit-filled growth. He instituted new programs, and even though the church was growing at a steady 10 percent yearly rate, true revival eluded them. Alec couldn't help thinking he was doing something wrong.

One night at home, while getting ready for bed, he pulled out a book that had been lying under his bed for six months in his I-must-read-this-one-of-these-days stack. The book was Paul Yonggi Cho's *Successful Home Cell Groups,* and Alec decided to read the first chapter to help put himself to sleep: "I started about 10:30 and read the first chapter. Then I decided to read the second chapter, then the third and the fourth. At three in the morning I finally finished the book, and I was so excited I couldn't sleep. I got up and put in a telephone call to Seoul, Korea."[2]

The result was an hour-long conversation with Cho's private secretary and a plan to attend one of Cho's leadership seminars the following October.

He thought a good preparation for the trip would be to visit some churches in the States that had experienced revivalistic awakening. One such church was the Church on the Rock in Rockwall, Texas, which in three and a half years grew from a nucleus of twenty people to a congregation of 4,200 using Cho's principles. It seemed a good place to examine cell-group theory away from the Korean hothouse. So he and his wife flew to Rockwall for a Thursday-to-Sunday visit.

"The church was everything I'd heard it to be," said Rowlands. "Six hundred people at midweek prayer service. Vibrant, fun worship. Well-organized cell groups and care networks. I learned a great deal. But the key to the visit came from a direction I never expected.

"On Thursday evening the pastor came up to me and said, 'Why don't you join us for our prayer meeting tomorrow morning?' I said 'Sure,' and asked when and where. They met at six A.M. I was staying thirty miles away at a motel in Dallas and mentally calculated what time I would have to get up to attend. I decided to go more out of duty than enthusiasm. I was glad I did.

"About seventy early risers met in a small prayer room. We began with a ten-minute look into the Word—an associate pastor gave a study from Ezekiel on God looking for someone to stand in the gap. Then we dismissed and spread throughout the sanctuary for individual prayer. I found a pew and prayed. In five minutes I was done. Everyone else kept going, and I knelt there wondering what to do for the next forty-five minutes. Finally, at seven o'clock we joined in a group prayer and song and dismissed.

"I didn't feel anything spectacular happen that Friday morning. But all through the rest of that weekend as I asked questions about the church's ministry, the words I heard were about methods, but the melody was always prayer. The Holy Spirit began to convict me that I was trying to pastor my church in my own efforts and energy, and my commitment to prayer was marginal at best.

"Sunday afternoon the senior pastor, Larry Lea, took me to lunch and asked me what the first thing I was going to do back in Cedar Rapids. I didn't even have to think about it. 'I'm going to become a praying pastor,' I told him. That was what he wanted to hear. It was what they had been subtly trying to tell me all weekend but resisted saying outright because they are always afraid someone will view prayer as just one more magic program to turn a church around instead of the essence of a Christian's existence. I came back to Cedar Rapids resolved to become God's man in the gap at this church, knowing that the only way one can become that is to pray with all the force you can muster.

"I came home on a Monday and on a beautiful, sunny Tuesday I cleared my schedule at church, took my Bible and Paul Billheimer's book, *Destined for the Throne,* and went to Ellis Park to pray and meditate.[3] I sat in a secluded parking spot overlooking the river and read and cried and prayed from nine in the morning until four in the afternoon. It was a very mild version of Jacob wrestling with the Lord. The Holy Spirit told me clearly that I was at a crossroads in my ministry. If I would begin to see myself as a praying pastor and lead this church to a ministry of intercessory prayer, he would do abundant things beyond what we could imagine. I read Exodus 16 where the Israelites do battle with the Amalekites, and as long as Moses has his hands lifted in prayer, they win the battle. When he drops them they begin to lose. I decided that would be the paradigm for my ministry. I wanted to be a praying pastor and trust the Lord to bless us here.

"I came down off my mountain and gathered the elders and told them of my decision. I told them I was going to start setting aside large blocks of time for prayer and Bible study, times I wouldn't be available to anyone. They supported me 100 percent. Next, I presented my experience to the congregation on Sunday morning. I told them I believed prayer was the trigger mechanism for exploding the gospel in our community, both as a fellowship and as a community. They supported me fully."

Changes began to happen. In order to make Rowlands's prayer resolve easier, the deacons rented him a small office away from the church that he used for prayer in the mornings. Growth started almost immediately. Church had been averaging about 450 in Sunday morning worship attendance. After twelve months it was running slightly above eight hundred. The intensity of worship increased dramatically.

Individuals began to make commitments to the ministry. Harold Tyler, a silver haired, long-time member of the congregation, walked up to Rowlands after one morning service and with tears in his eyes handed him a check for $40,000. "If things keep on going this way around here, we're going to need a new building," he said. "Here's the down payment."

Rowlands hopes he is seeing the beginnings of revival. It's certainly nothing on the scale of what we read about in Finney's autobiography. Yet something is happening, and the city of Cedar Rapids is aware of it. Can this be a bellwether of what happens when church leaders begin to see themselves as men and women of prayer?

Alec Rowlands himself is cautious in talking about what has happened for fear it will be misinterpreted as egoism or as premature announcement of what he really longs for: full-scale revival. He has seen too many church leaders claim far more for their personal experiences than is justified. So why does he tell his story at all? "Because I can trace all the changes that have taken place at this church and in my life to a moment of truth when I decided to pray. At that moment, I began to see significant growth in my personal Christian walk."

Alec Rowlands doesn't claim to be a prophet and admits that his decision to become a praying pastor hasn't been a cure-all. A large, black bearded man, he speaks with a clipped British accent that exudes honesty and realism. When the phenomenal growth of the first twelve months slackened somewhat, he questioned his continuing commitment—was growth slowing because of the mornings he missed his prayer time or because he wasn't being sincere enough? Even with his strong commitment to prayer, Alec knows the first thing that gets curtailed when schedule pressures arise is his devotional time. Yet his commitment to seeing himself as a praying pastor has not changed.

Can we learn anything from Rowlands's experience? Are we witnessing a unique working of the Spirit here, or are there principles we can learn to help us become more effective prayers? Rowlands's experience is a moment-of-truth decision to commit his life to prayer. Is that the kind of thing that can happen to any of us, and if it can, is there a way to increase the chances of it happening?

Looking back, Rowlands sees four interconnected needs coming together in his decision to become a praying pastor, things that have changed the character of his ministry:

1. *He finally, fully connected God's anointing with prayer.* Rowlands's call to ministry was not an occasional thing. He felt a strong call from very early in his life. He was born and raised in South Africa where his grandfather was a freehold farmer in the late eighteen hundreds. His father and grandfather, a Quaker, did some evangelistic work among the South African Indians, and his dad pastored a Baptist church there for ten years before taking a Full Gospel church in South Africa.

"When my dad took that church, he didn't know it was corrupt to the core. The Sunday school superintendent was sleeping around, the church treasurer had his hand in the till, and attendance had slipped to fifty. My dad worked at the church for three years and ended up in the hospital with an ulcer.

"When he got out of the hospital, he called the family together for a conference and told us he was ready to quit. He and Mom had decided to go away for a month-long retreat of prayer and fasting. If things didn't turn around after that, he would resign.

"He came back a month later, and nothing happened for three weeks. Then one Friday night at a youth prayer meeting, God acted. We had a normal time of prayer and then gathered around the front in a circle to conclude the meeting. Those in the circle suddenly felt the power of God in their prayers, and they began to cry and confess sin. I was only twelve and didn't know what revival was, but when I read today about the Wesleyan revivals, the descriptions fit perfectly what happened in that church. By Sunday the church was full of praying people—the church held one hundred fifty and there were people standing around the walls and sitting in the aisles. Within eighteen months over five hundred people were attending, and we had a new building. For three years the church continued to grow before it leveled off in the early nineteen sixties.

"I trace my call to ministry and my commitment to revival to those early experiences. But somehow over the years I lost the direct connection between revival and prayer. My strong need to see revival here, coupled with that need for prayer forced me to it."

2. *He recognized his need for brokenness.* Since his prayer experience, the sense of brokenness, that attitude that Roy Hession in *My Calvary Road* calls an "indispensable precursor of revival," is more and more present in his life.[4] Hession wrote about the Christian and Missionary Alliance revivals of the late forties and early fifties and concluded that we can't have revival unless we are willing to admit we are as Ezekiel's dry bones.

Brokenness is one of the hardest things for church leaders to attain. After all, aren't we already giving our life to service? Doesn't the sweat of our church-building and people-nursing count for anything? Yet God is quite clear about the relative values of service versus holiness: "Listen you leaders of Israel. . . . Listen to the Lord. Hear what he is telling you! I am sick of your sacrifices. Don't bring me any more of them. I don't want your fat rams; I don't want to see the blood from your offerings. Who wants your sacrifices when you have no sorrow for your sins? The incense you bring me is a stench in my nostrils. Your holy celebrations of the new moon and the Sabbath, and your special days for fasting—even your most pious meetings—all are frauds. I want nothing more to do with them. . . . From now on, when you pray with your hands stretched out to heaven, I won't look or listen. . . . Oh, wash yourselves! Be clean! Let me no longer see you doing all these wicked things; quit your evil ways. Learn to do good, to be fair and to help the poor, the fatherless, and widows" (Isa. 1:10-17, TLB).

Brokenness is our recognition of our creaturely status before God. It is the realization that we are not able to make it on our own. It is the beginning of all good things in Christ.

Rowlands traces at least part of his recognition of his brokenness to when he became a head pastor for the first time. "I wasn't ready for the weight of responsibility that falls to the head man. If the ship had gone down in San Diego where I was an associate, it would have been Dick who took the brunt of it. Here I'm the person responsible. Add to that the strong feeling among the people here that something should be happening in this church soon, and you can see the reasons for the pressures I put on myself. It finally resulted in my recognition that only God can make a ministry work. We only obey him.

"I remember what Moses said: 'If your presence doesn't go with us then don't take us from this place.' There were times in my ministry where I operated as if I thought, 'If your presence doesn't go with us, it doesn't matter because we can still make it on our own.' I blush to think about my ministerial arrogance of years past."

3. *He felt a need for a bedrock organizing principle in his life.* In addition to ministerial arrogance, Rowlands often felt overwhelmed by the sheer volume and diversity of tasks a pastor must perform in a growing church. This is not an uncommon feeling. When church leaders are asked to name the greatest hindrance to their prayer life, time pressure ranks number one. Rowlands's longing to simplify his life was always at loggerheads with his internal demands to accomplish great things for God.

Prayer has changed that. Prayer has become the greatest time management "technique" Rowlands has discovered. Prayer has become the standard against which everything else is prioritized. "I don't feel as if I'm running in a hundred different directions all at once anymore," he says. "I'm committed to the idea that I can do everything else exactly right and still be dead wrong in God's eyes if I'm not praying. Prayer has simplified my life, even though I'm doing as much, if not more, than before."

Several dynamics are at work in Rowlands's experience. Psychologists have long recognized the need for consistency in our minds between what we believe to be true and what we do.[5] If we believe prayer to be a high priority item, for example, and then behave as if a score of other things are more important (by neglecting our prayer time), our satisfaction in doing any of them is greatly diminished. It is as if we become subconsciously disillusioned with our own inconsistency. Few church leaders argue prayer's primacy; even fewer *act* as if that's true. When we do bring our actions in harmony with our convictions, a tremendous weight is lifted from our subconscious which no longer must struggle mightily to balance these two discordant elements.[6]

For Rowlands, the change has not made him an organized efficiency expert. He still has to be flexible. For example, when his office away from the church had to be given up due to financial pressures at the church, Rowlands blocked time out of his schedule each morning for his devotional life. From 9 A.M. to 10:45 he is not disturbed except for emergencies. Thirty to sixty minutes of that time is spent in personal prayer, the rest in Bible study and clearing his mind.

Rowlands is not fanatic about keeping a minute-by-minute schedule: "The church secretaries are glad we've got a computer now because I keep changing my schedule. What I've tried to do is prioritize broad responsibilities: prayer first, private study of the Word second, sermon preparation third, corporate prayer fourth, administrative tasks fifth. Every fourth week or so I total up the time I spend in each of those areas and make sure they rank in that order. If they don't, I make adjustments."

4. *His people relationships have also improved.* "One problem in particular had been nagging our staff. I finally decided I couldn't put off confronting the staffer any longer. Yet on the day I chose for the confrontation, the Lord very clearly told me, 'I'll take care of this, Alec.' Sure enough, that staff member came in and told me he recognized his bad attitude, and we worked it out. It was a beautiful resolution of a problem.

"People in the congregation tell me they've sensed a change in me. (It makes me wonder how bad I was before!) They seem more than willing to follow my leadership. They are very warm. I trace my increased sensitivity to the fact that I pray for them more diligently now. You can't pray for someone and not increase in your appreciation for that person. As Billheimer says in *Destined for the Throne*: nobody can be saved unless someone is praying for them.

"Since we've started our focus on prayer, people come up and say, 'I've never been so hungry to study the Word since we started praying together for that hour at church on Friday morning.' And people are always talking about how their private family lives have been revitalized through their commitment to prayer. Just last week we had a couple who had been unfaithful to each other come to the church for a marriage rededication ceremony, complete with tuxedos and all. It was a moving experience.

"People on their lunch hour come and pray in the sanctuary. It's been tremendous. It's made me feel closer to them and them to me.

"I don't want to paint an unreal picture. We still don't have unanimity on every decision. I have come to not expect it. I agree with Peter Drucker that if you have unanimity you haven't looked at the question accurately. Until you uncover some disagreement and process it, you haven't looked at the question thoroughly enough. I've come to accept the fact of carnality in the congregation. Not everyone is at the same place on their spiritual journeys.

"Perhaps my biggest comfort came from talking to Paul Yonggi Cho on that trip to Seoul. His is a magnificent ministry, but what I remember most is Cho looking at me once during our visit with very tired eyes and saying, 'You know, some mornings my flesh is just unwilling to endure the hours of work and prayer necessary to be faithful to this ministry. I get very tired. To not see answers to prayer and to still persist—that's the real test of faith.' That meant more to me than anything else I saw in Korea."

On the desk in Alec Rowlands's office sits a computer terminal where he writes sermons, letters, an occasional article. Leaning next to the desk is an eight-foot shepherd's staff, used once a year in the youth department's Christmas pageant. The old and the new symbols of ministry, perhaps.

But what characterizes Alec Rowlands's ministry more than either of those is a plaque that hangs by the side of his desk, a gift from his father by whose desk it hung for years in South Africa. It reads, "Prayer Changes Things."

Alec Rowlands pastors the way he does because he believes that is true. His personal decision to be a praying pastor made the difference.

TWELVE

TIMES, PLACES, AND PEOPLE

Reading habits are conditioned by three factors: the existence of privacy, the purchase of books by adults, and the presence of at least one adult who reads frequently.

C. S. MEDINA

A single day spent in your Temple is better than a thousand anywhere else. I would rather be a doorman of the Temple of my God than live in palaces of wickedness. For Jehovah God is our Light and our Protector. He gives us grace and glory. No good thing will he withhold from those who walk along his paths.

PSALM 84:10, 11

Once the decision has been made to pray, the time and place we decide to pray, and the people we associate with, all become crucial.

Carl Hines, a communications engineer for the Santa Fe railroad in Topeka, Kansas, credits some of these physical elements for stimulating his prayer life:

"I grew up in a home with a Christian mother and went to church regularly until I was five or six years old. But Mom got cancer and died when I was nine. Dad was an alcoholic, and we moved around a lot. I was bitter. From that point on, I moved far from the Lord."

He was searching, however, and when he moved back to Topeka, the need for a spiritual life became unbearable. His marriage had begun to deteriorate—his whole world seemed in danger of collapsing. Then he found Fairlawn Heights Wesleyan Church:

"I'd heard Pastor Ed preach once, and I remembered his name. So when I needed someone to talk to, I thought of him. I drove to the church. I had only visited the church once; I didn't know who to ask for. But someone there remembered me and called Pastor Ed. He and Pastor Tom came over to talk.

"Right there I made a commitment. It was December 3, 1981—an important date to me. As I look back, not a lot changed right then—and it didn't help my marriage at that point. My wife and I continued to argue. Over the next two years I was in and out of our house about four times.

"But in May, my wife asked me to come back home. It's been a little over a year now that we've been back together. I can't say all the problems are gone, but it's getting better, and I have confidence in the Lord that it will heal all the way.

"One of the constant areas of growth through all this has been my prayer life. I didn't really know how to pray. I still don't, I guess, in a final sense, and I pray daily that the Lord will teach me to pray better. Several things have helped. Our pastor, Tom Kinnan, started a prayer program, which has made my prayer life better in a number of ways.

"One, I can talk to Pastor Tom, and he can explain some of the hard questions I have about praying. Two, I have a prayer partner. When things are going bad, I can call George Fultz, and he'll pray for me right over the phone.

"I also like the prayer vigil. Someone is always praying— we're trying for round-the-clock coverage. My time is 1:30 to 2 A.M. At 1:30, the person with the shift before mine calls me and prays with me over the phone. Then I pray for a half hour and call the next person. It's quiet, and it's easy to be worship-ful at that time in the morning. It's helpful to know that I am one part of that program and that there are others before and after me who are carrying on the vigil of prayer.

"I have other specific places and routines that stimulate me to pray. I pray first thing in the morning while I'm still in bed. I also pray at my desk at lunch hour. My Bible's in the top drawer of my desk, and I simply open it and read it during lunch.

"There are times when I flat don't want to pray. I'm tired or I don't want to get up and do it, but I made this commitment and I say, 'OK, Lord, I said I'd do this, and I'm going to pray, but I need your help to do it.' The Lord honors that.

"I don't want to leave the impression that I've got it all

together now, but when I look back at the problems I had before and the ones I've got now, the ones now are nothing. I've seen great things happen through prayer both for me and the church. The church has grown because of the prayer vigil, the prayer chains, and the prayer-partner programs. And I've had some great personal answers to prayer.

"The biggest was during the worst part of my marriage. I wasn't handling things too well. I didn't want to go to a counselor, but I needed to talk to somebody. So I arranged to see Pastor Tom, but my wife wouldn't go. I was at work one day, praying about it, and I said, 'Lord if there's any way possible, let me and my wife come together for this counseling.' I knew the minute I prayed that something was going to happen. I'd prayed the same prayer before, but somehow this one was different. Within twenty minutes my wife called and asked if she could come to the counseling, too. The counseling session did not go particularly well, but I was amazed that within twenty minutes, and as hard as it was between us, that she came at all."

Several factors entered into Carl's decision to become a praying person. Certainly the time was right. The Spirit of God working within Carl had created a sense of need. His job was in a state of flux, and his marriage was on the ropes. It was a time when he could really learn.

He also came across a body of believers in the process of dedicating themselves to the ministry of prayer. The Fairlawn Heights Wesleyan Church was filled with people talking about prayer and looking for others to join them in their rededication to prayer. By joining this group of people, Carl enhanced his own enthusiasm for it.

Thirdly, the physical places of church, desk, and home as places to pray regularly contributed to Carl's development as a praying person.

The Teachable Times

Common wisdom tells us we're more open to learning at certain times than others. Parents learn this quickly. One night I took my son David to the White Sox baseball game and had a great time. The next morning, however, his mother asked him how he liked the ball game. He said, "It was great, except Dad didn't buy me a second Coke."

As a parent, I have begun to learn I can react to such complaints in nonproductive or productive ways. It's nonproductive to get angry or even to be disappointed by such a response. It's productive to see these moments as teaching opportunities.

I explained to David that the reason that I didn't buy the second Coke was that little people cannot satisfy their desires in an unlimited manner because they have limited funds. If I were to sit down and try to communicate that lesson at just any time, David would not understand it. When especially thirsty for a Coke, however, he listens carefully. I may not convince him of my argument's validity—certainly not when a second Coke is involved—but he will remember the argument and, if it makes any sense, *someday* make it his own.

The same is true of prayer. Prayer can be taught at certain times; other times it cannot. Trying to convince someone that prayer is necessary in an abstract setting is difficult. However, tie the need to crucial decisions, and the lesson sticks.

Is there anything we can do to create times of openness to prayer? Some come only through the circumstances of life and can't be simulated. Others, though, can be enhanced by placing ourselves in the position of learner about prayer. Or playing the role of prayer counselor to others.

Take, for instance, a study done with twenty chronic smokers who wanted to quit. Each was asked to play the role of a physician trying to counsel a lung-cancer patient to give up smoking. After attempting to articulate the arguments against smoking to someone else (the same arguments they had heard from others for years), the twenty subjects were far more open to changing their own ideas about smoking. They began to believe formerly ineffective arguments.[1]

Christian leaders find themselves in ideal positions to create times where the prayer habit is a topic of discussion. Rather than feel guilty about counseling others about an area where we might feel weak, we can view such counsel as an actual aid to our own practice.

Gib Martin, pastor of Trinity Church in Burien, Washington, runs a Bible class on Wednesday nights that he calls the Derelict Bible Study: "One of the prerequisites of the course is that we all call ourselves 'derelict' in this area. That way there's no posturing, and we all start out on even footing. Then we teach each other and learn more in the process."

A second way to stimulate teachable times is to create cues that trigger prayer behavior. For example, we have all been irritated by people who set their digital wrist watches to beep on the hour or half hour. (There's no better way to fight the irritation than to get a watch of my own—with the loudest beep I can find—and give others a bit of their own medicine.) But "beeps" during our day can be reminders to pray, a call to a short time with God.

We can create in our own lives several of these cues to tell us it is time for prayer. The bells in the old European monastaries rang six times daily as "cues" to prayer. Because of our erratic schedules today, we've put the church bells on our wrists. Perhaps there are other cues we could create to further sanctify our time.

Martin Cossins, pastor of Calvary Baptist Church in Monroe, Michigan, uses the times he awakens in the middle of the night as cues that something needs to be prayed about: "Sometimes someone or some specific need is on my mind and I pray for that. Other times I just use the fact of waking up as a cue to pray."

Both natural and artificial cues can be used as signals to short times of prayer.

The Place of Prayer

In one sense having a special place to pray is not important. We notice a startling variety of places in Scripture where prayer takes place: in the temple (Acts 3:1); in private rooms (Acts 1:13, 14); at house meetings (Acts 2:42); in prison (Acts 16:25); at the river bank (Acts 16:13); on the waterfront (Acts 20:36); and even by letter (1 Cor. 1:4).

For most people, however, a special place for private prayer is helpful. Henri Nouwen tells about the importance to him of the *poustinia*. *Poustinia* is a Russian word that means hermitage.[2] Nouwen has applied the concept of hermitage to his everyday living. While teaching at Yale, he lived in an apartment with a huge walk-in closet. Being a priest, he had a limited wardrobe and no need for that much space. He converted it to a prayer closet.

"The simple fact that I'm in the closet means I'm praying," he says. "I might have a thousand things to think about while I'm in there, but the fact that I'm sitting in this physical place means I'm praying. I force myself to stay there for fifteen minutes. I do my best to center my mind and clear it of distracting thoughts and get down to prayer, but if after fifteen minutes I haven't been entirely successful, I say, 'Lord this was my prayer, even all this confusion. Now I'm going back to the world.' "

We do learn to identify places with certain actions. The study of the relationship between a people and their environment is called human ethology. Church consultant Lyle Schaller thinks ethology has much to offer church planning. It can help us understand our attachments to places and enhance our spiritual discipline.[3]

It may sometimes be helpful to pair prayer with some other activity location. My wife recently bought an exercise bicycle. On the bicycle's reading stand she puts a Bible and her prayer list. Thus, while doing her daily fifteen or twenty minutes of pedaling, she also reads the Bible and prays through her list. Our spare room has become her *poustinia*.

Praying Companions

When pastors were asked who their role models had been for their prayer life, they most often mentioned a praying father or mother.

But praying parents cannot be chosen. Not everyone will be so blessed. And for the grown Christian leader, help must be found from among current groups. Perhaps the group with greatest potential is other pastors. Such a group would have been very helpful to Jim Davey, who noted that when he was a young pastor twenty-five years ago in Mansfield, Ohio, he would have profited greatly by having other pastors with whom to pray regularly.

The Christian leader can also be helped vicariously through other people totally absorbed in prayer. Watching people in the congregation grow in their prayer life, for example, can be stimulating.

Thomas Kinnan, whose church helped Carl Hines, has profited much from his church's involvement in prayer:

"When we started the program two years ago, I told my people my dream for the church was to see them in cloisters praying for one another after every service. My dream was to have them praying for one another over the phone, to have people asking me, 'Pastor, can you pray for something?' My dream was to have everyone talking about prayer and praying for one another so much that a critical mass was formed and we would become a praying church in every sense of the word.

"We instituted our programs and within the first five weeks, our average attendance increased by fifty-three people. Further, and I know this will sound strange, but we have great worship services every week. Now I know I don't preach a great sermon every week. But the people think I do, and I attribute that to prayer. Because we pray for one another, we have drawn together in an atmosphere of mutual encouragement and love. The people pick me up even when I'm not doing my best."

Fairlawn Heights Wesleyan Church sits about a mile south of the Menninger Clinic on the west edge of Topeka, Kansas. It's the edge of town that's growing, absorbing much of Topeka's white-collar growth. The large A-frame building is lighted by windows set at oblique angles to keep out the hot Kansas sun. But the church is more than a building; it's an oasis of prayer on the edge of the prairie. Carl Hines was attracted to Fairlawn Heights by the caring, praying attitude of the people.

"Carl came because we are a praying people, and he saw this as a place of prayer. We've made a conscious effort to come across like that to people in our community. We initiated P.R.A.Y.E.R. (People Responsive and Yielded Experiencing Results) Program to show our priorities. It's revitalized the people and the ministries here. Those who commit themselves to prayer are involved in any or all of the six different areas:

Prayer Partners. Two people who commit to pray for and with one another. They also become spiritually accountable to each other.

Prayer Corps. These individuals pray daily for the needs of the church as well as praying nonstop throughout all the services.

Prayer Chain. Emergency needs of people are sent through the network of other people who have committed themselves to pray immediately.

Prayer Vigil. From 8 P.M. Saturday night to 8 A.M. Sunday morning, people have committed themselves to half-hour time slots for prayer.

Prayer and Fasting. Designated meal times for people to isolate themselves in the presence of the Lord for constant, consecrated prayer instead of eating.

Prayer Bulletin. In order to keep the current needs of the church before the people, a weekly prayer bulletin is sent out to everyone committed to prayer. "We believe the more specific the requests the more specific and powerful the prayers will be," says Kinnan.

"Answers to prayer have been abundant, ranging from spiritual conversions to physical healings to material blessings. We have seen significant, tangible growth in all areas of the church: attendance, new Christians, and financial giving. A new vibrancy, a spirit of expectancy, permeates the services."

A place to pray and people to pray with are tremendous motivators to consistent, regular prayer. What really happens? People are encouraged and the mysterious adventure of prayer is reaffirmed.

Prayer is an excitement. We're on holy ground when we pray. There are amazing possibilities in prayer. Through it we can influence the principalities and powers of the universe. One man with God can conquer the world. That's the kind of adventure that needs to be inserted into prayer, and we can do it only by encouraging and building up one another in the practice.

THIRTEEN
I AM A PRAYING PERSON

Religious leaders are predictably more religious than any other leadership group. Ninety-five percent say they frequently engage in prayer. Scientists are the least religious group. Twenty-seven percent of them say they frequently engage in prayer.

CONNECTICUT MUTUAL LIFE REPORT

In the Navajo Indian language, the word most often used for prayer is a synonym for "holy person." For the Navajo, prayer cannot be understood apart from a person praying.[1] Prayer is a person acting to recreate the original oneness of God and man.

One of the keys to establishing a consistent Christian prayer life is to become a praying person—and to see yourself as a praying person. Prayer is not a religious act divorced from an actor. It cannot be compartmentalized. It must be part of a person's self-perception. Until then, prayer will always be a dreary duty rather than a self-identifying action.

Sometimes this is a slowly developing awareness. Sometimes it happens almost overnight—like it did for Jerry Cook, a Foursquare pastor from the Pacific Northwest:

"I had a heart attack last year and spent a good deal of time in intensive care. One night I was hanging on the edge of life, and looking back, I find it fascinating the things that were of no comfort to me as I was bumping into death.

"My accomplishments, for example. Pastor of a big church, author of books, world traveler—all the things that had made up the activity of my life before the attack. They didn't give me peace. I didn't consider them unimportant; I just didn't identify them as eternally important when eternity was staring me in the face.

"That surprised me because I remember thinking that being pastor of this good work for God, this church, faded in importance when compared with my Savior awareness. The thing that gave me the most comfort was that I was up to date in my relationship to Christ.

"Even after I recovered, that lesson profoundly affected me. For one thing, it called into question everything I do as a Christian leader. I did a kind of zero-based budgeting with the way I spend my time, and although it didn't change my actions as a pastor very much, it did change my perception of their relative importance. I made some lists: What are my most important investments in life? What are my important investments? What investments are unimportant?

"I also became more present oriented. In the past I might not have gotten as much out of this time talking with you as I could have. Since my illness, I find myself enjoying what I do right now as much as possible. I'm not always thinking of what I have to do this afternoon, or next month, when I should be maximizing what I'm doing right now.

"Many younger pastors have asked me how they can avoid a heart attack. They all want to keep operating at a thousand miles an hour and yet heart-attack-proof themselves. I tell them I heart-attack-proofed myself—I exercised, ate properly, had physicals—and it didn't prevent mine. I ask them to consider two things: In your intensity to do the work of the kingdom, are you placing the faith itself first or the form of the faith? If you are putting the church ahead of the faith, that's a red flag. It will lead to stress and frustration.

"Then I ask them to consider this: Do you want to invest your life in maintaining the form of the Christian church? Or do you want to invest your life in the spiritual well-being of the body? Both are important, but one always comes first in your thinking. Which one is it for you? Then I relate that my heart attack confirmed for me that my concentration should be on the second—which means I need to see myself as a humble pray-er not a super pastor.

"My prayer life is a time of fellowship with God. It has intensified since my heart attack, and I think much of it has to do with being grateful for life. Also, I learned dependence in the hospital. As I was lying in intensive care, I felt helpless, and helpless doesn't feel good. Someone had to brush my teeth; someone had to roll me over; someone had to help me go to the bathroom. I recognized my dependence on God.

"Out of that I have continued to feel closer to God, developing what I call lifestyle praying: I walk with God at all times, though at certain periods it intensifies. I keep a prayer diary that I review periodically. I have morning prayers and afternoon prayers. But basically I want my prayer life to be reflected in the whole way I live my life. Christ is present with us now. That's not mystical, but it is sacred. I want my whole life to revolve around the sacred."

Jerry Cook experienced a revamping of the way he viewed himself. His core perception was changed from "activist pastor" to "praying person." Psychologists tell us that such a reordering of self-perception is essential if longstanding habits are to be changed. If we think we can do something, or if we see ourselves as people who normally do such a thing, we are more likely to do it.

Such self-perceptions are determined by two factors: our own desires and the pressures of our environment. Who do we want to be? And what do people around us think we are? What do they think we should be?

Christian leaders generally want to view themselves as men and women of prayer. But sometimes the pressures of their environment do not contribute to that perception. Followers often assume their leader's prayer life is healthy but do not help nurture it. Will Sanborn, associate pastor of Highland Park Evangelical Free Church in Columbus, Nebraska, asked a group of pastors to rate the most important personal characteristics they need to bring to their ministry. They rated the top five as:

- Love of God
- Servant's heart
- Good prayer life
- Bible knowledge
- Love of people

Sanborn also asked what the pastors thought the members of their churches felt were the most important characteristics in a pastor. They thought the top five would probably be:

- Speaking ability
- Good personality
- Outgoing person
- Bible knowledge
- Love of God

"Good prayer life" dropped from number three to number sixteen.[2]

These pastors' perceptions may reflect a frustration they have with combining their prayer life and ministry. They rate prayer as an important component of ministry, but they do not feel supported in that perception by the people they serve. Other studies have shown that when the expectations of the leader and those of the followers don't match, frustration is bound to result. It is evident that pastors don't feel as supported in their commitment to be praying pastors as they could be. How does a Christian leader come to the place of seeing himself as a praying person?

Sometimes it does take a life-threatening experience. Like Jerry Cook, those who have them testify to the soul-searching produced, which often results in a changed perception of self.

For many others, the perception comes more gradually. Subtly, prayer becomes the focus of life rather than a duty tacked on at the beginning or end of the day. Until it becomes lifestyle praying, it will be a frustration both to the Christian leader and the people he or she serves, who must be shown the fruits of a commitment to prayer.

What are the fruits of lifestyle praying? First, the praying person is innocent of guile. No hidden agendas in prayer, no ulterior motives. The praying person is one who learns the hidden mysteries of the kingdom through conversation with the King. Remember Jesus' prayer in Matthew 11: "O Father, Lord of heaven and earth, thank you for hiding the truth from those who think themselves so wise, and for revealing it to little children."

Not only is honesty a fruit of lifestyle prayer, but honest prayer also helps make us praying persons. When asked, *What does God really expect of you in your prayer life?* the answers of Christian leaders rarely took the form of how many more minutes they should pray. Far and away the most frequent response was "God wants me to be honest with him." John Newman once said in a sermon, "To be totally honest is to be already perfect."[3]

Second, the praying person seeks God's mind. As Matthew 6:7, 8 reminds us, "Don't recite the same prayer over and over as the heathen do, who think prayers are answered only by repeating them again and again. Remember, your Father knows exactly what you need even before you ask him." The praying person is looking for an answer to one question: *What does God want in this?* Not *What do I want God to do for me?* The joy of discovering that what God wants in our lives makes us the most effective, fully functioning Christians we can be moves prayer from the status of pious act into the realm of communion with God.

That kind of commitment reflects itself in leadership tasks. Business meetings consider God's will the focal point of decision making. Sermons and addresses reflect a searching for God in the secular lives we lead. Interpersonal relationships operate on biblical standards rather than manipulative technique. Such wholesale commitment, rare as it is, will be noticed.

Third, there are times when the praying person recognizes that nothing but prayer is the thing to do. Satan's attacks vary in intensity. They never exceed that which we can bear, but they do sometimes require all the spiritual power we can muster. The praying person sometimes needs to draw apart to concentrate all energies on God and his power.

The Holy Spirit does indeed answer the sincere searchers and fill them with the power to become praying people—in God's eyes and their own.

F O U R T E E N

DEVELOPING A PLAN

Problem solving takes five steps: (1) general orientation; (2) problem definition; (3) generation of alternatives; (4) decision making; (5) verification.

D'ZURILLA AND GOLDFRIED

THE STEPS OF PRAYER
First, decide what you really want.
Second, decide whether the thing you want is a Christian thing.
Third, write it down.
Fourth, still the mind.
Fifth, talk with God about it.
Sixth, promise God what you will do to make this prayer come true.
Seventh, do everything loving that comes to your mind about it.
Eighth, thank God for answering in his own way.
Ninth, release the whole prayer from your conscious thinking.

E. STANLEY JONES

I am not gifted, but I can plod.
WILLIAM CAREY

Writer Derek Price reports that in the 1920s, practically every piece of research equipment in British physics laboratories was stuck together with red Bank of England sealing wax. The wax was the best cement then available for holding a vacuum. Researchers depended on the wax for almost all their experiments. In a sense, progress in physics depended on a substance developed for businessmen's correspondence not scientific experimentation; this red gooey wax determined what the finest minds in the golden age of physics could discover about their science.[1]

Prayer benefits from technique in a similar manner. The postures, memory aids, spurs, and other tools we use, like the red Bank of England sealing wax, can make the difference between what is possible in prayer and what is not. They can lead to a greatly enriched and deepened prayer life, even though they themselves are peripheral to it.

Unfortunately, each person's prayer life is so unique that no set of techniques works for everyone. Warren Wiersbe, Bible teacher with Back to the Bible radio broadcasts, said, "In talking to pastors and other leaders over the years, I've always tried to stress that everyone is led by God to prayer in a little different way. In fact, it often seems one person's approach may even contradict another person's approach."

We must develop our own techniques to fit the nature of our struggles and strengths. We must experiment.

Isolating the Problem

Christian leaders face different challenges. But despite the specialized circumstances, Christian leaders attribute their inconsistent prayer lives to four basic problems:

Not enough time. The most commonly mentioned problem. The root cause may be busyness or inefficiency, but many church leaders admit to their need for a course or two in time management.

Administrative jumble. A second commonly mentioned reason is the diversity of tasks the Christian leader must perform. Being pulled in several different directions at once can fragment concentration, making it difficult to center on God. Carl Lundquist, president of the Christian College Coalition, put it this way:

"The unpredictable daily schedule of a busy administrator has been my greatest single hurdle to regular formal prayer. Early breakfast meetings and late-night meetings have been devastating. When my family was young, I sought to overcome this by having an earlier dinner hour so we could have a leisurely time for prayer before evening activities. In more recent years, since the children are gone, my wife and I have practiced early morning prayer before we move into the day. But administrative tangle is still a problem."

Inconsistency. This problem is variously described as a lack of discipline, weakness of the flesh, or inconsistency. Jacques Ellul identifies it by saying "the first aspect of the combative nature of prayer is that we are combating ourselves. Through prayer man avoids anguish and the divided self, but to pray is the last action he can think to take to come out of his own tragedy and destruction."[2] Paradoxically, prayer is the answer to weakness of the flesh, but that very weakness keeps us from consistent prayer.

One pastor said, "It's so easy to shortchange my prayer life. I'll go to bed one night and suddenly wake up with a deep sense of guilt, and I'll realize I haven't been praying. I feel tense until I start to pray. I'm glad God does that to me, but it makes me realize how weak I am in the face of Satan's attempts to get me to stop praying."

Keeping freshness in prayer. Many leaders said they fell into ruts, patterns of prayer that over time became dishonest. "I think I should be praying for certain things, so I do. But my heart is in a different place, and the content of my prayers doesn't match where I am in life."

C. S. Lewis said in *Letters to Malcolm Chiefly on Prayer*: "It is no use to ask God with facetious earnestness for A when our whole mind is in reality filled with the desire for B. We must say before him what is in us, not what ought to be in us."[3]

You likely can identify with one or more of these problems. Your situation is more specialized, perhaps, but if you were to write out in one sentence why you have difficulty praying, the reason would probably fall into one of these categories.

Once you have identified your particular problem, what's the solution? You are probably willing to experiment with different ways of solving the problem. That's an important step: having the freedom to experiment.

It's not unlike the experimentation one goes through in adjusting to a mate. Over the years, my wife and I have discovered we complement one another in many ways. She is practical and detail oriented; I am idealistic and look for the bigger patterns. I like to teach; she would rather administrate. She's good with money; I buy unneeded gadgets. These differences need not lead to incompatibility; if seen as advantages, they make for a good marriage. Judy and I, however, often clashed over them early in our marriage.

We learned to perform relational experiments to turn the clashes into efficient divisions of responsibility. For example, early in our marriage, I handled the money, a responsibility I dealt with by not paying much attention to it. I didn't shop for the best values; I didn't search out the best interest rates; I didn't stop to think whether I should eat out for lunch or settle for a sandwich at home. (The problem was heightened by the fact that Judy was earning the money while I went to school.)

My lack of attention did not create knock-down, drag-out fights, but Judy could not understand my disinterest in matters financial. She realized we weren't on the poor-house doorstep, but she also knew we weren't being the best stewards of what God was giving us.

For a long time, we didn't do anything about it. It seemed quite normal and right to us for me to handle the bankbook.

We didn't change until Judy decided to buy a house. I didn't want a house, mainly because of the bother of it all. Judy wanted a house because it was a good investment for our future. After several months of disagreement, I said in exasperation, "If you want a house, you buy it." So she did—and in the process, took over responsibility for our money. And it has worked out very well.

We talk frequently about overall financial goals and decide together what they should be. Then Judy does the rest. Both of us feel better. I feel relieved of a burdensome responsibility. Judy has thrived with it because she, with her careful approach to detail, does not consider it a burden.

A similar reluctance to change is often at the core of frustrated prayer lives. Our prayer lives aren't that bad. We pray enough to get by and satisfy ourselves further by noticing no one else seems to do so well at it either. But in our most honest moments, we realize the relationship isn't all it could be. We know we aren't on the doorstep of hell, but this nagging guilt is keeping us on the defensive. This lack is in the one spiritual area that infects all the others.

Often we don't deal with it because we're not sure what to do. We have advanced beyond just giving thanks before meals and using a four-step formula for bedtime prayers. But most of us, upon careful reflection, would probably find that we are more bound up in limited technique and idealized prayer roles than we realize. The role models of prayer we had as young people and the corporate prayer our denominational traditions set forth influence us greatly. For me, it was whether or not to vocalize an "Amen" or "Yes, Lord" while someone else was praying, a practice I have come to enjoy and appreciate as a community-building exercise during public prayer. For you, it may be something else: a particular form of addressing God, a particular way of closing prayer, a list of behaviors permissible during prayer time. Some of these guidelines may be theologically motivated, but most are strictly cultural (like the man handling the household money) and can easily be modified or changed if it adds to the effectiveness and vitality of prayer.

Like the marriage relationship, our relationship with God needs constant care. Prayer is the communication vehicle through which our relationship with God develops. God is open to different ways of coming to him in prayer. Since our bond with God is strong enough to stand some experimentation, why not try some different approaches? It's likely some simple changes will, first of all, relieve boredom. More important, they might spur further growth and help us build on our personality strengths instead of accentuating the weaknesses. It has been said that "Prayer is to religion what original research is to science." In praying and exploring different ways to pray, we are doing the original research that will eventually contribute to spiritual maturity.

One caution is in order. When trying to fix something, such as prayer, we don't want to do more harm than good in the process. I recently heard about an action by the State Unemployment Office in Oregon. They went to a computerized system to produce checks for the unemployed residents. In seeking to more efficiently distribute money, however, they laid off two hundred workers, thereby contributing to the very problem they were trying to solve.

Any similar adjustments we make in our life of prayer should be done with the realization that our problem probably is not that extreme and that minor tinkering rather than major rebuilding is what we need.

Techniques to Combat the Problems

What are the possible solutions to each of the major problems of prayer? As we have seen, much depends on individual temperament. Some, for example, are inspired by reading of lifestyle praying, such as Brother Lawrence's *Practice of the Presence of God*.[4] Others may be more attracted to the disciplined approach, such as Ignatius Loyola's *Spiritual Exercises*.[5] Some want to know how to structure that early morning hour to make maximum use of their devotional time. Others call God to mind for ten-minute stretches throughout the day.

Following are ideas and techniques gleaned from church leaders in each of the four major problem areas. The ideas are meant as shopping lists rather than prescriptions. They are listed as idea sparkers—you must translate each to see if it fits your particular life circumstance, if it needs some modification to fit, or for some reason does not fit at all.

Lack of Time

Fitting prayer into a schedule already overcrowded with the organizational demands of ministry is difficult. Several simple efficiency hints can help.

Many revolve around scheduling prayer as a regular appointment. Logan Sparling, pastor of Christian Life Fellowship, Greentown, Indiana, said: "As a pastor I depend heavily on my appointment book. Each appointment is carefully entered and diligently kept. One day while feeling guilty of my own prayerlessness, I concluded that I did not spend time with God because I didn't consider it as important as the other appointments in my book. I decided prayer needed to be scheduled on a daily basis. I began to enter those appointments in my book. After several weeks of diligently following my plan, my prayer life became a joy. My divine appointment is the most important one I have each day."

Fred T. Hall, pastor of Central Christian Church, Sherman, Texas, uses a daily reminder sheet to keep him on schedule: "It's headed with the title 'Things I Must Do Today' followed by the date and fourteen numbered lines. The first item I enter each day is prayer. I try to do the things on top of the list first."

One of the added values of such scheduling is that of record keeping. Because the appointment with prayer is written down, it is easy to see if the appointment was kept. Positive or negative trends in prayer time can be accurately gauged. Psychologists call such practices "self-monitoring." Counselors who use this approach with patients discuss the importance of accurate record keeping.[6]

Benjamin Franklin kept a little moral account book where he daily recorded his ethical successes and failures. The book was essential to his scheme, for it not only enforced daily self-examination and thus daily renewal of his efforts, but it also measured growth just like an accountant records credits and debits. Franklin carried the book with him all his life.[7]

There are other ways to fit prayer into an extremely busy schedule. Roger Janke, pastor of Our Father's Evangelical Lutheran Church, Greenfield, Wisconsin, said that once he realized you can pray with your eyes open as well as shut, there were many additional times he could pray in the midst of his schedule: standing in line for the cash register, riding the bus, waiting for someone else's tardy arrival, while doing dishes.

Another pastor, Robert Bundy of Northwoods United Methodist Church, Jacksonville, North Carolina, said his most effective prayer time was while driving. He described his prayers as bullet prayers lifted quickly to God for action on others' behalf.

Dave Zehring, pastor of Covenant Baptist Church, Mesa, Arizona, uses stoplights as times to pray. He gains an additional benefit—he used to be frustrated at being slowed down by stoplights. Now they are positive motivation to pray.

Vic Pentz, a pastor of First Presbyterian Church of Yakima,

Washington, prays while watching the television news. "While watching the news, an inevitable feeling of helplessness about the human needs depicted on the screen causes me to pray silently for them. It's a way of lifting up the problems of the world to the Lord when I probably wouldn't take the time otherwise."

Another way to fight the demon of busyness is to recognize that even within the busy times of ministry, prayer opportunities arise. Lowell C. Strumpfer, pastor of First Alliance Church, Lakewood, Colorado, finds some of his deepest times of prayer during sermon preparation. "The urge to fall before God in the midst of reading or studying the Scripture is the one exercise in prayer that has stood out above all others for me in my thirty-five years of pastoral ministry."

Administrative Jumble

Lack of time is not always the problem for Christian leaders. Sometimes it's the confusing diversity of tasks they must perform. Most leaders do not have a consistent schedule from week to week, and the confusing array of tasks can inhibit consistent prayer. Even Jesus was plagued with this problem. Different interest groups constantly besieged him: the sick wanted healing, the questioning wanted counsel, the opposition wanted incriminating statements, his immediate aides wanted policy decisions. His way of coping? To frequently withdraw to a quiet place.

Today's Christian leaders often do the same. Chilton Knudsen, pastor of St. Benedict's Episcopal Church in Bolingbrook, Illinois, spends one day each month at a nearby retreat center. She tries to clear her mind of problems and refocus on the broad goals of her church's ministry.

Lynn Scovil, pastor of Plymouth Church, Oshkosh, Wisconsin, retreats one day a week to the local library where he doesn't check out books but takes time for quietness before God.

Retreat isn't always possible. Many Christian leaders have

developed ways to carve out time in the midst of being pulled six different directions at once. Several said they use a verbal cue of some kind to facilitate the switch. R. Stewart Wood of St. John's Episcopal Church, Memphis, Tennessee, pairs his prayer with a mental stimulus of praise that is a cue to begin: "Closer are you than breathing, nearer than hands or feet." Stewart notes that this helps him be still and simply listen for God and acknowledge his presence.

Martin Luther in his famous note to his barber, Peter Beskendorf, on how to pray, tells a similar story of something he used to initiate his prayer time. "I take my little Psalter, flee to my room, or, if it is during the day and there is an occasion to do so, join the people in the church, and begin to repeat to myself the Ten Commandments, the Creed, and if I have time, some sayings of Christ or verses from Paul and the Psalms. This I do in all respect as children do."[8]

Some harried church leaders use the jumble of their ministerial atmosphere to good advantage. They wed the tasks of ministry to their prayer life. Perhaps the most overarching approach to this kind of prayer was one developed by Harold Ockenga, long-time pastor of Park Street Church in Boston. At one point in his life, Ockenga was commuting almost weekly from Boston to Pasadena, California, in his dual role of pastor at Park Street and president of Fuller Theological Seminary. "I've always been very busy, but I feel there is a secret. My secret was administration by prayer. For forty-one years I have kept everything on a detailed prayer list:

- I kept problems on there—when I went over it daily I was reminded by the Lord if I hadn't done anything about them. Problems with my family, with our evangelistic outreach at the church, with the faculty at Fuller, everything went on the list.

- I kept a list of people I disagreed with on my prayer list so I could pray for them, asking the Lord to change the situation between us. Many times the Lord forced me to either mellow my position or seek rapprochement in some way.

- Of course, I also kept special requests on my list.

"When any of these prayers were answered, I would just write answered across the notation and then I wouldn't look at that entry again.

"Keeping this list kept me alert to my responsibilities, the chief one being my need to bring everything to God in prayer."

Dan Cole, pastor of Rio Grande Baptist Church, Terre Haute, Indiana, uses the occasion of praying for people to also write a note of encouragement to them. This strengthens his prayer life and establishes a written relationship with them through the notes.

Richard Foster, author of *Celebration of Discipline*, learned to pray in church committee meetings when he was a pastor: "One of the things I quickly learned was silence. I didn't always have to speak and didn't always have to control the meetings. I took the opportunity to silently pray for people as I watched them interact. It was exciting for me to see some of their heaviness lifted as the meeting progressed."

Pastor Arthur Maendl said he infused his prayer into his gardening chores: "I have found no better place to pray than when I'm mowing the grass. The noise from the mower drowns out all other sounds, and no one ever bothers you when you're mowing the lawn."

Inconsistency

Weakness of the flesh attacks all of us. And as Paul notes in Romans 8, there is no way to overcome our lower natures but the power of the Holy Spirit. Utilizing the Comforter's power can be helped by three common techniques.

First, accountability. Many Christian leaders make themselves accountable to others for regular prayer. Sherm Williams, former pastor of Fremont Community Church in Fremont, California, developed what he called a prayer support team made up of members of his church. He asked one person to be responsible for each day of the month. At a weekly meeting, the seven men responsible for that week would meet with Williams at breakfast. Sherm would give each a three-by-five card outlining his schedule for the day of the week assigned to them: "I not only listed my schedule, but I would list a personal need and a ministry need that I felt I needed prayer support for. The men would also give me a three-by-five card with their schedules and their needs listed. Sometime during the day we would pray for the day's partner.

"The results were meaningful. Often my prayer partner for the day would be just the person I needed prayer from; or it would be a day when they needed the particular prayers of their pastor. The group also became the prayer base of the church and heightened the entire church's awareness of the fundamental necessity of prayer. My wife had a parallel accountability group of women, which gave her an important prayer support base also."

Chester E. Larson, a district superintendent for the Evangelical Covenant Church, phones one layman each day of the month as a prayer partner for that day.

Thomas Kinnan, pastor of Fairlawn Heights Wesleyan Church in Topeka, Kansas, has a designated person call him at a time he has set aside for prayer. He then must face this individual as well as the Lord about whether indeed he is praying or not. Kinnan does this on a limited basis—when he feels his prayer discipline is getting weak.

Jane Feerer of Grace Episcopal Church, Waverly, New York, and Christ Episcopal Church, Roseburg, New York, has covenanted to meet twice a day with two separate groups of parishioners. One meets at 6:30 A.M. and they walk two or three miles. Another meets at 5 P.M. and they go through the Episcopal service of evening prayer: "Meeting with others keeps my prayer life consistent and keeps me honest." Edward Lyman, priest of St. Joseph's Roman Catholic Church in Friendsville, Pennsylvania, has a group of close friends and parishioners that meets weekly at the rectory to offer prayers, sing hymns, and give praise to God. "Praying together with others at a set time insures taking out the time from a busy schedule because others as well as yourself depend upon it."

What all these leaders are doing is establishing a contract between two or more people that has prayer as its required fulfillment. Some of these arrangements are simply understood. Others are formalized with a written covenant to pray for one another. For many, writing out the words of the exact agreement is helpful. We live in an age when that kind of written agreement is increasingly accepted. Prayer contracts can be very simple covenants—"I will pray for you" or "I will pray at such and such a time"—or they can outline more specific prayer guidelines. Much depends on the purpose of the contract and the level of help desired.[9]

Weakness of the flesh can also be attacked by providing positive and negative reinforcements for prayer. One pastor, Scott Meacham of Valley Baptist Church in El Cajon, California, wrote that he set aside each morning for prayer and "would not eat a meal of physical food until I first have some spiritual food and prayer time. Food really motivates me personally so I make sure I get my prayer in every morning through this means."

Weakness of the flesh can also be combated by turning prayer into a physical act. The advantages of physical exercise are obvious and currently popular. Many Christian leaders talked about praying while jogging, swimming, walking, or riding bicycles.

Other physical aids are also useful. One frequently mentioned was the prayer journal. Daniel Berger, pastor of First Baptist Church, Fessendon, North Dakota, said, "I date each entry in my journal, then write out at least a part of my prayer. I find this keeps me going to the Lord daily because the empty pages look like blots. It's a way to keep me reliant on God's grace to change myself." Richard Jessup, principal of Mountlake Christian School, Everett, Washington, also writes out his prayers: "It's clear to me that there's a tremendous value in this when I think that Augustine, Thomas à Kempis, Peter Marshall, and a host of other well-known spiritual leaders have done the same."

Some pastors have a bit more formal method, combining Bible study with journal keeping. Calvin Elifson, pastor of Highland Hills (Illinois) Bible Church, reads a passage from the Bible, identifies a thought that impressed him from that passage, and writes it in a Bible reading record developed by the Navigators. Then he prays. "If I miss a day of Bible reading and prayer I see it in my record and am reminded to be more consistent."

The most frequent form of physical exercise mentioned in the Bible is fasting. R. A. Torrey, in his book *How to Pray*, says: "If we want to pray with power, we should pray with fasting. This, of course, does not mean we should fast every time we pray, but there are times in emergency or special crisis when men of earnestness will withdraw themselves even from the gratification of natural appetite that they may give themselves up totally to prayer."[10]

Fasting is not as popular today as it was in biblical times. In a society where *proper* nutrition has become almost a god, *no* nutrition, even for a short period of time, seems almost a blasphemy. Of course, the body can easily go without food for days without any adverse affects.

It is true that fasting is not commanded in the Bible, but many men in the Bible, including Jesus, fasted and gained spiritual benefit. Fasting is frequently mentioned in conjunction with prayer, especially prayer at times of special withdrawal and spiritual retreat. It should be considered a valid, even desirable option for accentuating the spiritual experience of prayer.

There are many other physical ways of focusing attention during prayer. Robert Brown, pastor of Round Lake Baptist Church, Gladwin, Michigan, says he prays out loud because it keeps his mind from wandering. John Vertefeuille, pastor of Church at Lakewood, Tacoma, Washington, prays while standing up and walking around: "I have my prayer items written on three-by-five cards, and I flip through them as I'm walking. I haven't fallen asleep even once doing this." Robert Munger, associate pastor of Menlo Park (California) Presbyterian Church, also paces while he prays. "I talk with God using this body language to express my petition. It not only keeps me awake and alert but reinforces the fact that I am talking to a living God who is present, powerful, and listening."

The obvious goal of all these practices is to associate prayer with something positive or something beneficial to help overcome the lethargy that can strike us all.

Keeping the Content Fresh

For some, knowing what to pray about for a long period of time is the biggest hurdle. We can't pray about everything, but it is very helpful to have some plan of attack regarding content.

The most common way of solving the content problem is to keep a prayer list. Steve Brown, pastor of Key Biscayne (Florida) Presbyterian Church, has kept a prayer list for the past fourteen years. Its major elements are family concerns, prayer needs of church officers and staff, and a list of ministry associates he feels a special closeness to. One section of the list is a bit unique, however, and illustrates some important principles he uses in deciding what goes on his list: "I call it my hit list. On it are people that I am out of sorts with for one reason or another, and I just can't think of any other way to deal with them except pray.

"For example, several years ago a pastor here in Miami was doing very well, and I found myself jealous. For me, that was a perplexing problem. Ordinarily when I have a problem with someone, I go and talk it out with that person. But the sin of ecclesiastical jealousy is awful—it would kill me to admit that sin publicly. So I put that pastor on my hit list. After praying about it for weeks, I was able to go to that pastor and say, 'I want you to know what's been going through my mind. You don't have to respond to it, but I just want to confess it to you.' Then we ate lunch and didn't say anything more about it. And I haven't had any problem with it since."

Interpersonal problems and jealousies will always be with us. As Marshall Shelley demonstrated in his book, *Well-Intentioned Dragons*, dealing with problem people is a fact of life for local church leaders. And some of the problems don't disappear easily, if at all. Some are so persistent and reconciliation proof that there is nothing to do but give them up to God. Steve Brown has found prayer to be a key in these situations:

"I guess the hit list is my way of saying, 'God, I've done my best with this situation and haven't resolved it; please help me.' It's been good to see the way God has honored the list. As I pray for people they gradually get removed from it—I honestly believe that the only way most people get off the list is because I prayed for them. It's not a long list, usually, never more than ten or fifteen names. Right now I'm in the eye of the hurricane because there's nobody on it. No one ever knows if they're on it or not, of course. A couple of times I have announced from the pulpit that I have removed another name from my hit list, and the congregation has applauded. But I rarely do that because I don't want people wondering whether they're on my hit list or not. I really want it just to be a way for me to hold up special interpersonal problems before God and get his help with them."

There are many other creative ways of using a prayer list. John Barr, pastor of First Church of God (Anderson), Neodesha, Kansas, divides his prayer list into two sections. First, he keeps those things that he wants to pray for every day. In section two he divides it into six different areas, each representing a different day of the week. Each day lists a topic for the day: non-Christians, Christians within the church, fellow ministers, family members, etc.

Larry Troxel, pastor of Our Redeemer Lutheran Church, Quincy, Illinois, divides his membership list into seven sections, praying for one section each day. Larry Pillow, pastor of Second Baptist Church, Conway, Arizona, places one fruit of the spirit under each day of the week and asks God to make that one fruit a reality in his life for that particular day.

There are, of course, more formal divisions and prayers one

can use. Paul Moser, rector of Emanuel Episcopal Church in Bel Air, Maryland, uses the daily morning and evening prayer published in the Book of Common Prayer as the content of his devotions. He and his wife pray through them together: "Since we have four children, seven to seventeen years of age, we found that the church building is the best place for the two of us together. We open the church at 7:30 A.M. with Morning Prayer and close it at night with Evening Prayer. This does many things for us. It gives us a sense of shared ministry about the church and also lets us listen to one another in our prayer time."

Another church leader organizes his prayer time according to subject in morning and evening. In the morning he focuses on God and his guidance and praise for his family. At midday he focuses on thanksgiving and requests that he keeps on four-by-six cards in his Bible. In the evening he and his wife pray for Christian organizations with which they are involved. Other pastors divide prayer time into sections of so many minutes each, concentrated on a particular subject such as praise, thanksgiving, confession, petition.

Another pastor, Edward Schuit, an area representative for Africa Inland Mission in Waynesboro, Pennsylvania, combines his prayer time with junk mail. "Like many Christians homes, we receive many appeals for financial aid. Obviously we cannot respond financially to all of these, so we use each mailing as a prayer request. They are piled beside our breakfast table. A typical morning will find us praying for Columbia Bible College, Jews for Jesus, Greater Europe Mission, and missionary Mary Smith. We feel it's a real ministry."

During the week, Steve Moldenhauer walks around his sanctuary praying aloud for people who usually sit in particular pews. "I look at a particular seat and remember the person who sits there. Then I walk behind the pulpit as I pray and ask for special blessing on the message. Sometimes I pick up a hymnal and read some titles or verses to jog my memory in other areas of need. This has become a special time in my ministry."

Selecting the Alternatives

Obviously, there is no shortage of techniques. Indeed, we are more often paralyzed by having to choose one idea out of so many many options. We're reminded of Moses standing on the banks of the Red Sea as the Egyptian army was bearing down on him. Moses was sure God would do something and told the whining Israelites so. Yet as Moses stood confidently on the banks the soldiers drew closer and closer. Finally, God found it necessary to tell Moses to get moving: "Why are you crying out to me? Tell the Israelites to move on. Raise your staff and stretch out your hand over the sea to divide the water" (Exod. 14:15,16).

The time comes when we must quit ruminating over what to do and act. What factors need consideration?

If a counselor were helping you, he or she would probably start by thinking, *This is such and such a type of patient, who needs this particular kind of therapist, using that method of treatment, thus yielding the best outcome.* This is called a prescriptive view of counseling. It operates on the assumption that most treatments can not be classified as "good" or "bad" in any final sense. Instead it holds that different treatments and therapists may be appropriate for some patients but not for others.[11]

A similar dynamic works for prayer. Three variables need to be considered in selecting a prayer style:

Content. The appropriateness of the content of prayer is determined by its compatability with scriptural truth. If it is not filled with Christian content, it won't work for Christian prayer.

Personality. H. B. London, a Nazarene pastor in Salem, Oregon, said, "I never understood the attitude of pastors who get together and pray. Almost automatically the whole personality of the group changes, and they begin to groan, 'Oh God, help us poor miserable sinners.' I'm not trying to be the least bit irreverent, and I'm not arguing against my need for help and my sinfulness, but the worm-such-as-I attitude just doesn't fit my personality. My personality is more joyful, and when I'm on my knees I can say with confidence, 'Oh God, help me.' It seems to me that one's prayer life and prayer practice should fit his or her personality; that's what I strive for in mine."

Method. The method needs to be one that will make it useful for the one praying. Trying to read a Bible in German, for example, is not useful content to one who doesn't know German. Singing hymns, for another example, is not useful to one who dislikes singing.

The method must solve the particular problem you have with prayer. If inconsistency is the problem, and you are a person who relates well to friends helping you, a prayer partner may be the answer. Doc Kirk noted that he welcomes accountability: "Many times I have called up someone and said 'I would just like you to check up on me in my prayer life. Please ask me, whenever you see me, how it's going or give me a call if we don't see each other very often.' It just takes five minutes and it's very helpful to keep you on track."

On the other hand, you may not relate well to someone checking up on you—or such a person may not be available. For you, a specific length of time in prayer may be a stimulating goal. The method should be chosen based on what you feel comfortable with and what you will chafe at the least.

Choosing the right method may be almost instinctive. You seem to know what you can handle and what you can't. Choosing might be similar, perhaps, to the function the human brain plays in choosing what we eat. Richard Wertman in an article in *The Technology Review* noted that the human body produces chemical messengers (called serotonins) that tell the brain what the body doesn't need. For example, the brain may say that the body is well stocked in carbohydrates and doesn't need to choose those kinds of food anymore. A person's appetite reflects the message.[12]

Similarly, a person's "comfort level" with a certain style of prayer may be a pretty reliable indicator from the Holy Spirit about what style to use. The danger of adopting the "if it feels good, do it" mentality must be counterbalanced by the first consideration that the technique being considered is scriptural.

It's likely that a significant amount of experimentation may be necessary. But don't lose patience if some of the things you try don't work. Some good advice about prayer experimentation might be "Do something quickly, but don't be in a rush as you do it."

Verification

The final step in solving the prayer problem is to make sure it's working. The criteria are not hourly standards set by someone else but the sense of increased faithfulness in your own spiritual life. If faith isn't growing, prayer isn't working.

Marti Ensign, an associate pastor at the Free Methodist Church in Seattle, Washington, frequently reevaluates her prayer style: "On a regular basis I check up on my prayer life. If it's not an effective force in my life, I don't hesitate to change and use different methods to get in contact with God. I don't want to get stuck on one style just because somebody told me it works. My needs may change. A prayer list may have worked for me five years ago, but now it doesn't, so I try something else. Over the past few years, I've used hymns, I've tried different physical postures, and I've tried long periods of solitude and silence. After reading some books on spirituality recently, my life went into a more meditative pattern for awhile. I've also done a lot with prayer groups—right now I'm involved with two. There are a lot of different ways to communicate with God, and I'm one who needs variety."

Ensign's comments on variety point to a larger truth about the prayer experience. Knowing God is a total experience that calls every facet of our personalities into relationship. We don't know him in just one way. Thus, it's unthinkable that we can gain maximum fellowship by just using one method of prayer.

I've probably driven by Madison, Wisconsin, fifty times. It's halfway between my parents' home in St. Paul, Minnesota, and my current residence in Wheaton, Illinois, so we frequently stop there for a meal. In our traveling rush, we have never gone to downtown Madison, several miles from the freeway; we have always chosen a restaurant off the interchange. My impressions of Madison, therefore, are relegated strictly to the commercial tangle by the freeway.

Prayer life can suffer similarly. We can get so wrapped up in doing prayer one specific way that we don't get a full view of what it can mean to our spiritual lives. One perspective can limit our understanding and ultimately inhibit the faithful growth that needs to take place.

FIFTEEN

RED FLAGS OF PRAYER DISORDER

A soul untried by sorrows is good for nothing.

THEOPHAN THE RECLUSE

To win one hundred victories in one hundred battles is not the acme of skill. What is of supreme importance in war is to attack the enemy's strategy.

SUN TZU

There are two perils to be avoided. One is emotional unreality and the other is intellectual preoccupation. There must be truth as well as spirit in all worship, and nowhere is the combination more necessary than in the secret place of prayer. Altar fires are kindled and quickened by truth, but the truth must get to the altar.

SAMUEL CHADWICK

A colleague recently returned from a summer vacation at his in-laws' farm in central Kansas. In between stints of hoisting bales of hay from baler to flatbed truck, he got a chance to philosophize with his father-in-law.

One of the more profound insights to emerge was on the different outlooks of farm folk and city dwellers. This from a man who both farms and works in a farm-implement factory in town: "The biggest difference I can see is that city people always think that this year has got to be better than last year. If they don't get a raise, acquire something new, or find themselves somehow better off, they think they're failures.

"Farm folks look at things a bit differently. We know there are going to be good years and bad years. We can't control the weather. We can't prevent a bad crop. We can't control sickness. So you learn just to work hard and make up your mind to take what comes."

When it comes to our spiritual lives, most of us are city dwellers. We discourage easily. It doesn't take too many setbacks before we're overwhelmed with our failures, and weeks can slip by before we dig our way out to start again. We'd be better off if we accepted slippage as part of the territory.

David has to rank near the top of any list of biblical pray-ers, yet his spiritual journey was anything but smooth. Second Samuel records the roller-coaster ride his development takes. In chapter six, for example, he pleases God by bringing the Ark back to Jerusalem. But then he gets in a fight with his wife, Michal. In chapter seven he approves a plan to build the temple recommended by the prophet Nathan. But then we discover that he failed to check with God to see if it was all right. In chapter eight he subdues the Philistines and the Moabites, and he generously invites Saul's grandson Mephibosheth to live in the palace. But in chapter ten he commits adultery with Bathsheba and arranges Uriah's death. God never abandons David, but that's because David always repents and tries again. We see great growth continue throughout his reign, but it's growth punctuated with periods of failure and decline.

For any of us, spiritual growth is not a steadily increasing incline but more of a bumpy climb. Overall improvement is visible when seen from a distance—but it's hard won and uneven. And too often the setbacks dominate us.

Prayer is an important key in this roller-coaster ride. John Piper notes that "prayer is the barometer of your spiritual life. It measures your sense of absolute desperation and dependence on God." It's important that we keep a close eye on such an important measuring standard.

Properly watched, prayer can help us anticipate and counteract problems before they get too serious. We should expect down times, but we should also be alert to spot and remedy them before they get the best of us and set our spiritual life back too far.

Fortunately, there seem to be common tipoffs that everything is not going well in one's prayer life. Following are the eight most common red flags.

When You're Irritable with People

The most common answer Christian leaders give to the

question, *How do you know when your prayer life is slipping?* is "I get irritable with people." It's interesting that the status of the most intimate relationship of our lives, the one we have with God, reflects itself in our relationships with people.

"When I get short with the church secretary, I know I need to pray more."

"Counseling is always a burden, but when I start to view the problems people bring to me too judgmentally, I know I'm not praying enough."

"My wife can probably tell you best when my prayer life is getting shortchanged—I begin to shortchange her."

A sister problem to irritability is insensitivity. When we're preoccupied with ourselves and our problems, we miss what's going on in the lives of those around us. People hurt, and we don't see the pain. The trapped look in our associate's eye, which betrays a marriage gone sour, is unnoticed. Prayer makes us slow down and notice what's going on, not only in our own psyches, but in those around us. Pray not, think not; think not, see not. We go on our narrow path, blind to needs we could otherwise help meet.

Paul Rees talked about what his prayer time does for his people contacts: "Frequently while I'm praying, a name will drop into my consciousness that I hadn't thought of for months. I instantly recognize that I should be praying for that person. I become more aware of needs in those closest to me, also. It's almost as if God is helping me rehearse what I should be doing for people."

When You Find Yourself Conforming Not Transforming

Fred Smith, in his book, *You and Your Network*, notes that one of the dangers of our peer relationships is the pressure to conform to their standards rather than offering them the opportunity to be transformed by the gospel of Jesus Christ. His loose paraphrase of Romans 12:2 is "Don't be molded from the outside but have a set of values that forms you from the inside out."[1]

Watch your relationships with people. Are you consistently conforming to their attitudes, or do you see them adopting the Christian attitudes that God is making manifest in your life? If you see more of the former than the latter, chances are you need to pray more. One pastor notes that the by-products of too little prayer are clear in his life: "I have too much preoccupation with what people might think of me rather than what God is thinking of me. I worry about human assessment of my ministry rather than God's assessment. When my prayer life is solid, I'm able to lock in to God's will quickly and carry out his intentions, human success notwithstanding."

When Prayer Lacks Urgency

Prayer is warfare. Sometimes the battle is open conflict. Other times it's cold war. But we must never lose a sense of the enemy. If Satan is not real to you, that's a red flag that your prayer life is not what it should be.

Satan is more than a red-caped figure who occasionally inserts himself into human affairs by trying to buy a soul or corrupt a church. The action of Satan is pervasive. Helmut Thielicke has rightly observed that "behind all the dangers in our life and behind all the dark menaces that overshadow it, there is a dark, mysterious, spellbinding figure at work. Behind the temptations stands the tempter, behind the lie stands the liar, behind all the dead and the bloodshed stands the murderer from the beginning."[2]

Evelyn Christenson in *What Happens When Women Pray*, writes that people having trouble with their prayer lives rarely talk about Satan's opposition. Biblical and historical prayer giants always talked about the war between good and evil. The most active prayer comes out of talking about and resisting Satan.[3]

If prayer is indeed the quintessential Christian activity, then it stands to reason that it is the one activity Satan abhors most, and he will attack it with utmost effort. Satan's strategy in attacking the kingdom of God is to discourage prayer. We can lose battles in this war—in an imperfect world, Satan will win many. But we must be extremely active in the warfare over our own spiritual lives.

One pastor said, "My struggle in ministry is to preserve and maintain a wartime mentality. The threat to my church and my own spiritual well-being is a deceptive sense of peace and prosperity and comfort. We're in a war, and the stakes are eternal. I want my people to feel the crisis. The front lines are bloody; Satan is winning massive victories all over the world. I pray daily that the Lord will keep me alert—with all my weapons poised—so I never come to a Sunday feeling dulled about what I have to do."

When You Don't Feel Your Prayers Are Being Answered

Christian leaders believe in answered prayer. Few leaders would deny the positive activity of God in their ministries. But sometimes the *feeling* that God isn't listening starts to creep into our minds. That can be the beginning of skeptical, and thus ineffective, prayer.

The problem can be accentuated by an inability to accept a negative answer. Too many of us see negative answers as no answer at all. In this scheme, a positive answer is a real answer, the only answer. A negative answer is a mistake.

God's answers, however, are answers—whether positive or negative.

The Bible is full of instances where God answered prayers in the negative. Moses prayed to see the Promised Land. God answered no (Deut. 3:23-29). The army of Israel prayed fervently for victory over the army of Benjamin in Judges 20:19-28 and God gave the Benjaminites a bloody, awesome victory—a negative answer, according to God's unknown wisdom.

One pastor remembered his experience as a boy: "I always wanted to be a major league baseball player. I prayed daily that God would grant this deepest desire of my heart. A lot of kids have that dream, I guess, but I carried it further than most; I was good enough to play minor league baseball and kept at it until I was twenty-eight years old, when I realized I wasn't going to make the majors. In some ways, I felt like God didn't answer my prayer. But as I continued to pray, I realized he was just answering my request negatively, and was leading me to seminary and eventually into the ministry."

Child-rearing experts say that children thrive in an atmosphere where they know where they stand. Tell them yes, tell them no, but tell them. The poisonous effects of uncertainty are far more damaging than the temporary sting of disappointment.

Prayer is similar. We need answers, but we should be able to accept negative ones. The question is how. One possible help toward accepting is to keep records of all the positive answers we receive. God does provide and remembering those provisions salves disappointment. Warren McFarlan in *Computer Decisions* writes that when a major blunder is committed in a well-run business, one way to protect against the fallout is to keep records and other concrete evidence of past achievements.[4] This puts the failure in perspective. Without proof of day-in-day-out excellence, those stung by the mistake are too likely to focus on the negative. This bit of boardroom advice, translated to our prayer lives, is a good rationale for keeping answer books, either mental or written, of our prayer requests.

Jim Danhof of First Covenant Church, Cedar Rapids, Iowa, said one of the red flags of his prayer life was failure without reason: "There's failure with reason. You look back and say, 'I see what I did wrong.' But if I hit a stretch where there's failure and no obvious cause, that means I had better get my prayer life going. The power for ministry is in prayer.

"I've just gone through a period of failure without apparent reason. For a couple of years now we've done some exciting things: moved into a new building, doubled our budget, grown by 20 percent, and written a doctrinal statement. But the last six months everything I touched turned to disaster, and I couldn't figure out why. I became introspective and depressed. I realized I had to return to prayer, and soon the answer came. I was developing a martyr leadership style where I wanted everyone to feel sorry for me, and I'm convinced it was due to lack of prayer."

When You Are Dry

All of us in ministry face dry times, the times when we have nothing to say and five pressing engagements where we must say something. We sit down to prepare and the Lord doesn't speak. The Bible may as well be written in Chinese, and prepackaged sermons seem a worse alternative than ever. Even prayer, if we have enough discipline and resolve to see to it, provides little relief.

It's at these times we learn the meaning of the word *duty*. We accomplish out of duty. The perfectionistic motors our hovering mothers started in us at age three come in handy. Or it may be our sense of call. For some it may be the simple commitment to a task, or guilt about accepting a paycheck. Whatever it is, we carry on somehow. But the words come from preaching engines that seem not to have been oiled.

Perhaps these dry periods are payment for the lack of prayer six months ago . . . or six days ago.

Often our dryness comes from what C. S. Lewis called the "error of Stoicism," by which he means that because some days we have intense, spiritually rewarding experiences with prayer, we come to think that we should feel that way every day.

But when dryness comes, our prayer life is the first place to look. One pastor said, "I discovered early as a preacher that if I didn't keep up my prayer, I lost the attention of the people. If you don't pray and get blessed, then you don't have that mysterious something that makes people listen. Prayer makes Scripture come alive for other people as they listen to you."

During the dry periods, it's important to remember that God continues to work through us even though we don't feel like he is. Andrew Murray said that the Holy Spirit works through us most powerfully when we feel the worst about our prayer life.

When Your Work Is in Disarray

Consistent prayer brings order to life. It gives us a sense of priorities. Without prayer we find ourselves deluged with many unrelated demands. Prayer orders those demands; it gives us direction.

When prayer is slighted, we find ourselves floundering. Priorities become unclear. Efficiency dips and we begin to doubt our skill and competency. One Christian leader said, "When I let prayer slip, I find a lot of emotional garbage begins to accumulate that I'm not aware of. It slips below the surface, and before I know it, I'm depressed."

What to do? One pastor recommended that this is the time for a sermon on prayer: "For some reason, when I feel my prayer life getting away from me, preaching on it helps bring me back. And of course, it's good for the congregation also."

When Apathy Strikes

The most obvious red flag is when you feel apathetic toward things spiritual. Older writers on prayer often called this "leanness of soul." We don't feel close to God, but don't feel any particular need to be close either. We feel slightly depressed, out of touch with God, out of sorts with the world.

In evaluating the cause for apathy, the first thing to consider is health. Is there a physical reason why discouragement has set in? Another factor recently being studied is the influence of the body's biological clock. The body has a natural way of adjusting its internal clocks, which order the daily peaks and troughs in a variety of bodily functions. For example, the body reacts differently at six A.M. in the winter than it does at six A.M. in the summer.[5] A preset time for prayer may find the pray-er approaching quiet time with different emotions than at another season. Expectations and prayer methods may need to be altered or else the different feelings may be interpreted as apathy.

If physical causes are eliminated, the spiritual cause can be considered. One pastor who occasionally has suffered with apathy says, "Nothing happens externally. My preaching is OK. People in the congregation don't notice anything. I get to work on time. My wife notices a kind of disengagement; I sense an enormous loss of joy. I know what the problem is: I have shifted over from God's power to my power. It happens subtly, but once I rely on my power system, I get drained fast, and that's when apathy sets in. I ought to be more sensitive and catch it sooner, but I'm not. The only way I can break out of it is to get away and do some concentrated praying."

When You Feel Good About Your Spiritual Progress

This may seem like an odd red flag. Why should I be cautious when I feel good about the way my prayer life is going? The answer is that grace works secretly in our lives. The closer we draw to Christ, the more work we see that needs to be done in our lives. This should not be cause for discouragement—God's grace is sufficient. But neither should it be a cause for an unbalanced euphoria. Our pride is sufficient to tip us over just when we find ourselves walking too tall. We don't have good enough vision to see our own progress. We are far too prejudiced.

Paul Toms, pastor of Park Street Church in Boston, has said, "There is great danger in strength. The Scriptures are full of warnings: Beware when you have eaten and are full (Deut. 8:10-14). 'After Rehoboam's position as king was established and he had become strong, he and all Israel with him abandoned the law of the Lord' (2 Chron. 12:1). 'After Uzziah became powerful, his pride led to his downfall' (2 Chron. 26:15-16). There are many more references to the danger."

There is one fail-safe method to measure our prayers: to ask continually the question, "Am I doing this to please God or to please myself?" The minute we feel pride about our prayer life, we have ceased to be motivated by the proper source.

These red flags are warnings that our prayer life needs attention. Once a red flag is waved, our work may involve painful intervention, but it's better than letting the condition deteriorate further.

Gregory Wiens, pastor of Salem Church of God in Clayton, Ohio, tells the story of his five-year-old son, Jordon. "One day he ran a splinter into his finger and came sobbing to me. I asked him what he wanted done. 'I want God to remove the splinter.'

" 'But I can remove it,' I told him.

" 'No, when you do it it hurts,' Jordon explained. 'God can do it without hurting.' "

Jordon didn't realize that sometimes God entrusts responsibilities to human beings, and sometimes our treatment involves pain.

There's no avoiding the pain of being human, of being fallen. Discipline and obedience help us come to God in prayer. When we don't want to pray, we must recognize the rebellion as Satan's work. We must come before God and wait, saying, *You are my grace; you are my mercy*.

In his own time, God will speak. Until he does there will be some pain.

SIXTEEN

THE JOY OF PRAYER

Just as thieves do not lightly attack a place where they see royal weapons prepared against them, so he who has grafted prayer into his heart is not easily robbed by the thieves of the mind.

ST. MARK THE MONK

H

ow much prayer is enough? If "total minutes prayed" is not the standard, by what do we measure the quality of our prayer lives?

The question of quality struck me recently while jogging. I realized my nine-minute miles take over twice as long as the ones run by marathoners, and they run twenty-six miles compared to my three. I am not a marathoner and have no immediate intention of becoming one. So their standard means little to me except to remind me of increasing age.

But between gasping breaths, I decided I should be measured against *some* standard. If not an Olympic standard, an age-graded standard? (Average thirty-eight-year-olds run a mile in so many minutes.) A magazine editor's standard? A Christian jogger's standard?

Or should it be a personalized, subjective standard? How I feel afterward? Whether or not I maintain my ideal weight? My heart rate after running?

There are many scales against which I could be measured, but which is the right one? The question occupied me for a few blocks and, because I was working on this book, I transferred the question to the Christian leader's prayer life. What should we measure our prayer lives against? The time other Christian leaders spend in prayer? An age-graded standard? How we feel after prayer?

I had two problems to solve now, and the hard thinking slowed my jogging even further. Fortunately, the answer to my jogging dilemma came quickly. At what must have been the nadir of my running speed for that day, a mosquito landed on my cheek and bit me. Images heretofore held of me effortlessly flowing down the street, hair swept back by the wind, vanished, and I was left with the awful truth that I was running so slowly that an insect normally cowed by the faintest rustling of air could attack my bloodstream undaunted. My standard for running from that time forward became enough speed to discourage even the fastest flying mosquitoes.

The question of a proper prayer standard, however, remained. What is God's standard? What does he expect?

He probably doesn't expect us to compare ourselves against the Jesse Owenses of prayer. It is indeed admirable and inspiring that a few of our spiritual forefathers prayed hours at a time. It is praiseworthy that Martin Luther, for example, sometimes prayed three or four hours a day. But Martin Luther and others were spiritual marathoners, living in a different time and age, and God may or may not be calling us to the same practices.

The standard of our prayer lives in many ways is like two marriage partners getting together and deciding what kind of communication is needed to keep their marriage healthy and growing. That level of communication will vary from couple to couple; the nature of the communication will vary as will the topics discussed, the amount of time needed alone, and the amount of outside help needed to bolster the relationship. In a similar way, the number of minutes we spend in formal prayer is likely to vary from person to person.

But that is not to say a standard of some kind is unnecessary. It is. God expects each of us to fight the sin and apathy that have driven us apart since Eden. He recognizes our weakness in restoring harmony. So he provides us a power source that gives us strength to pray. That source, the Holy Spirit, excises the ulcerating sufferings of our souls and transforms them into God's language, prayer. "The Spirit comes to the aid of our weakness. We do not even know how we ought to pray, but through our inarticulate groans the Spirit himself is pleading for us, and God who searches our inmost being knows what the Spirit means, because he pleads for God's own people in God's own way; and in everything, as we know, he cooperates for good with those who love God and are called according to his purpose" (Rom. 8:26-28, NEB).

Our standard of prayer, then, is the degree to which we have opened the sufferings of our souls to the Holy Spirit. Three things tell us if that is happening.

If Faith Is Growing

It is true that the elements of faith can be known intellectually—we can understand what to do and how to do it, and we can understand the way God has operated in the world past and present. But without prayer, that knowledge will be unbalanced and incomplete. Jacques Maritain once said, "Intelligence itself can only develop its highest powers in so far as it is protected and fortified by the peace given by prayer. The closer a soul approaches God by love, the simpler grows the gaze of her intelligence and the clearer her vision."[1]

A healthy prayer life gives a sense of completeness to all the disparate elements that make up our lives. For the local church leader, the growth of faith is reflected in ministry itself. The tasks of preaching, counseling, and administration become clearer and more purposeful. They begin to fit, instead of seeming like things-to-do that pile on top of one another in the leader's daily schedule. It's the clarity R. A. Torrey was talking about when he said, "Three things happen when ministers pray: they will have a new love for souls, a new faith in the Bible, and a new liberty and power in preaching."[2]

Not only do the tasks of ministry take on a new clarity, but they fit together in a whole. Ministry becomes a single-purposed calling instead of a hodge-podge of good works. Sherm Williams notes that his staff prayer times helped keep balance in his ministry: "One of the real dangers for a pastor is spending all his time in one area of ministry: out shepherding the flock, or evangelizing the community, or studying in his office, or whatever else his specialty happens to be. In our accountability group, we would tell one another what we had been doing, and we each checked each other for balance."

Growing faith means life becomes more and more oriented around our spiritual center. Perhaps no better description of the person of growing faith can be painted than that given by Thomas à Kempis in his classic work, *The Imitation of Christ*: "He who tastes all things as they are, and not as they are reputed and reckoned to be, this man is wise and instructed more by God than men. He who knows how to walk from within and give small weight to things without, does not wait for places or times, for devout exercises of devotion. The spiritual man quickly gathers himself together, because he never squanders himself wholly on external things. No outward labor, or occupation, at the moment needful, stands in his way but as events turn out, so he adapts to them. He who is rightly organized and ordered within, is not concerned over the wondrous and perverse doings of men. A man is hindered and distracted, as he draws things to himself."[3]

A Desire for More Prayer

The cumulative effect of prayer should be to desire more. As a group, Christian leaders reflect this desire. When asked on a survey how many minutes they prayed per day, 50 percent said they averaged fifteen minutes, 20 percent said they averaged thirty minutes, 5 percent said they averaged sixty minutes. When asked, *How many minutes a day would you like to pray?* those who averaged fifteen minutes a day most often answered they would like to pray thirty minutes, those who said thirty minutes answered sixty, and those who prayed sixty said they'd like even more.[4]

The desire for more, though, isn't an indiscriminate desire for quantity. It should be a longing for more time with the Father, but time balanced by the desire for deeper levels of prayer. It's much like the struggle a local church faces in balancing evangelistic efforts with discipleship. New members must be brought in, but existing members need to be discipled. The resources of the church must be allocated to accomplish both aims. Similarly, the resources of our prayer lives need to be allocated to accomplish the two standards of prayer: more time in formal prayer and the intensity of the time already spent. The desire for more should be controlled by at least two factors:

1. *More should not be interpreted strictly in terms of minutes.* In some instances, better prayer may come from spending less time at it. High bursts of energy can be sustained for only short periods of time, and if your personality is one that prefers short, high-octane bursts instead of longer, sustained efforts, less time may actually lead to more prayer. It's up to each of us to find the maximum point of effectiveness by weighing our intensity of prayer. The balance may change also with the circumstances of our lives.

Every once in a while while driving around the streets of a coastal city, you'll see a small boat on a trailer. The boat is only about twelve feet long and has unusually high gunwales, although at the middle of the boat they drop to approximately rowboat height. To my Midwestern eyes, this kind of boat—a dory—looks odd. It would be impractical on a Minnesota lake where the waves never get higher than a man's knee. But in the ocean, such height is necessary to keep the long, rolling waters out.

Some boats are built to handle heavy seas, some to skip around shallow lakes. Some prayer practices are designed to handle heavy loads of accumulated problems. Others are made to deal with bite-sized problems throughout the day. We allocate certain periods of prayer time to handle our current needs.

2. *There are definite physical limitations to the amount of prayer*

necessary. One pastor said, "I'm not sure an old man should try and run a marathon. He may kill himself trying. He probably should be satisfied with two miles a day. I realize that God expects as much out of me as I am able or capable of giving. But to make myself sick or to put myself down because of my inability to be a great prayer warrior is counter-productive. Each and every day we run the race with whatever we have to give, as we have strength, knowledge, and ability.

"For me a model that has always felt right was one I copied from a surgeon friend of mine. He got up at 5 A.M. and unhurriedly went down to his front room where he read, meditated, and prayed. Very relaxed, he thought through his surgery schedule and then went upstairs to dress. For him, that quiet time just sitting in his living room was his most productive time of the day. I've found it true for me also, but I realize others' needs may be different."

The idea of a regular time of dedicating everything to God, and then consistent effort throughout the day to relate everything back to him struck a responsive chord in most Christian leaders. A life of balanced dedication is the surest road to contentment. Perhaps Satan's favorite tactic is to throw us off balance even in the area of devotional practice. St. Vincent de Paul said, "Be careful to preserve your health. It is a trick of the devil, which he employs to deceive good souls, to incite them to do more than they are able, in order that they may no longer be able to do anything."

The Joy of Prayer

A friendly old clergyman, meeting Groucho Marx for the first time, remarked, "I want to thank you, Mr. Marx, for all the enjoyment you've given the world." To which Groucho replied, "And I want to thank you for all the enjoyment you've taken out of it."

Like many elements of our spiritual lives, prayer has taken a bad rap as a joyless experience. It should not be viewed so. In fact, one of the standards of effective prayer should be the joy it produces in our souls. Christian leaders are almost unanimous in their desire to somehow see the joy of prayer.

Jeff Ginn said, "I pray because I just like spending time with God quietly. I enjoy the experience of praying. The hardest part is simply getting started. I swim a lot for exercise, and the hardest part is jumping into that cold water. It's not a good experience at first. But after you're in and you're wet, you enjoy it. Prayer is similar. It is difficult to get started sometimes. But I attribute that difficulty to sin. The overall joy I get from prayer is overwhelming. The best thing for me and my ministry is to simply sit home with God and talk with him."

Jim Danhof said, "The weakest part of my prayer life is the discipline. I'd like to feel it isn't a discipline. I'd like to feel it's natural and enjoyable. It's odd that we call prayer a discipline when it is really a joy. I revel in the delight of prayer, yet recognize that I have to go through the discipline to reach the joy."

Perhaps we should not wonder that prayer can be difficult. It seems anything good takes an extra effort to accomplish. Samuel Taylor Coleridge said, "The act of praying is the very highest energy of which the human mind is capable. Praying, that is, with the total concentration of the faculties. The great mass of worldly men and of learned men are absolutely incapable of prayer."[5] Perhaps we should expect to pay some price in terms of comfort to expend the energy required. But the essential bedrock of joy should triumph.

The secret, perhaps, lies in viewing the overall relationship being developed with God as a long-range good that far outweighs any temporary difficulties and inconveniences. Gib Martin said, "In the last few years, prayer has become more than a doctrine. It has become a verbalization of a sweet reality. True prayer is built around the *Shema* of Deuteronomy 6:5: 'Love the Lord your God with all your heart and with all your soul and with all your strength.' I can feel that now. I know when my heart isn't loving God fully, and I know when my soul isn't loving God fully, and I know when my strength is being sapped by ungodly concerns. When I am in harmony with this verse, I can sense a wholeness; when I am not, I feel fragmented and pulled apart. Joy comes from the harmony prayer gives life."

The Greek dramatist, Aeschylus, noted one element of Christian prayer: "Pain that cannot forget falls drop by drop upon the heart, until in our despair there comes wisdom through the awful grace of God."[6] But there is another overriding element to prayer that supercedes even the despair that drives us to our knees. It is the knowledge that through prayer we are slowly, surely recreating the oneness with God that our impetuous sin eons ago destroyed. It is the knowledge that God wants that oneness, and if we will enter into partnership with him to attain it, the result will be joyous indeed.

There's a tribe in Kenya, the Masai, who many years ago were moved from their home to a different part of the country many miles away. In order to make the move less traumatic, the Masai took with them the names of their hills and rivers and valleys, and gave them to the hills and rivers and valleys of the new country. And although the new terrain may not have been as lush as the old, the Masai rested easier with the comfort of knowing their new home was in some ways similar to it.[7]

In prayer, we find ourselves seeking a lost oneness with our old home, the heart of God. We have been wrenched from that home by sin and now know an urge that drives us to reunion. Prayer satisfies that urge, for now at least. It is a renaming of our current longing with the title of the old perfect one. It is recognition that God has renamed hopeless sin. It is now forgiven sin. He has renamed powerlessness: power. Weakness: strength. Despair: joy. We are living on dangerous, foreign ground. The only way to survive is to claim what we can for God, and for the rest seek the peace only prayer can bring.

BIBLIOGRAPHY

Like prayer itself, a person's choice of books on the subject is intensely personal. The question, "What is your favorite book on prayer?" draws many different answers.

That shouldn't be too surprising since *Books in Print* currently lists over 850 being published on the subject.

Following are eight books on prayer, mentioned often by Christian leaders as helpful in their devotional lives.

Bloom, Anthony. *Beginning to Pray*. New York: Paulist Press, 1970, 75 pages.

Ostensibly for people who have never prayed before, this short book would profit even the most experienced. It raises the basic issues of what prayer is and what it means to pray to God. A classic. Written by an Eastern Orthodox archbishop.

Bounds, E. M. *Power Through Prayer*. Grand Rapids, Michigan: Zondervan Publishing Company, 1962, 87 pages.

Written to pastors, this is a powerful exhortation for leaders to pray without ceasing. What the church needs today, says Bounds, is not better preachers, but better pray-ers. The author was both a preacher and a lawyer.

Ellul, Jacques. *Prayer and Modern Man*. New York: Seabury Press, 1970, 178 pages.

The best discussion of the peculiar problems modern man faces in trying to pray. Man has always had difficulty praying simply because of sin. But modern man faces some unique cultural pressures. The author is a French theologian.

Hallesby, O. *Prayer*. Minneapolis, Minnesota: Augsburg Publishing House, 1975, 176 pages.

This book is currently experiencing renewed popularity. It follows a very structured, simple outline but is powerful in its truthfulness. It stresses the humility and simplicity needed for effective prayer. The author was a Lutheran seminary professor from Oslo, Norway.

Lawrence, Brother. *The Practice of the Presence of God*. Nashville, Tennessee: Thomas Nelson Publishers, 1981, 93 pages.

This is a book about lifestyle praying. It is a brief but powerful meditation on how to worship God in the midst of tedious work. The author was a dishwasher in a monastery in seventeenth century France.

Lewis, C. S. *Letters to Malcolm: Chiefly on Prayer*. New York: Harcourt, Brace and World, Inc., 1963, 124 pages.

A book of letters to a close friend on the everyday subjects surrounding prayer. It raises the most common questions about prayer and combines a beautiful writing style with an excellent sense of humor. The author was a Cambridge professor who became a Christian later in life.

Merton, Thomas. *Contemplative Prayer*. Garden City, New York: Doubleday, Inc., 1971, 116 pages.

This is mainly a discussion of prayer for those able to spend large amounts of time at it, especially those who would practice a full-time ministry of intercessory prayer. Some of the principles, though, are applicable to more ordinary forms of prayer. The author was a Trappist monk.

Murray, Andrew. *With Christ in the School of Prayer*. Grand Rapids, Michigan: Zondervan Publishing Company, 1983, 162 pages.

Thirty-one studies on the prayer life of Jesus. A classic, biblical study of what prayer means. The author was a Dutch Reformed minister in South Africa.

NOTES

PREFACE

1. P.T. Forsyth, *The Soul of Prayer* (Grand Rapids, Michigan: William B. Eerdmans Publishing Company, 1916), 11.

2. George Gallup, *Religion in America: Gallup Report Number 222* (Princeton, New Jersey: Princeton Religion Research Center, Inc., 1984), 71.

CHAPTER 1

Fyodor Dostoevsky, *The Brothers Karamazov* (Garden City, New York: Literary Guild of America, 1949), Part II, Chapter 3.

1. Terry Muck, "Ten Questions About the Devotional Life," *Leadership*, III,1 (Winter 1982): 30-39.

2. Quoted in Jacques Ellul, *Prayer and the Modern Man* (New York: Seabury Press, 1970), 114.

3. For a discussion of the history of Christian prayer see Joseph A. Jungmann, *Christian Prayer Through the Centuries* (New York: Paulist Press, 1978).

CHAPTER 2

G. K. Chesterton, *Orthodoxy* (New York: Dodd Mead, 1908), 16.

1. Federico D'Agostino, "Religion and Magic: Two Sides of a Basic Human Experience," *Social Compass* 27, 2-3 (1980): 279-282.

2. Genesis 5:21-24.

3. An excellent discussion of the effects of technology on the prayer life of modern man is found in Jacques Ellul, *Prayer and Modern Man* (New York: Seabury Press, 1970), 21ff.

4. George Koovackal, "Worship in Islamic Tradition," *Journal of Dharma* 3 (1978): 395-415.

5. Jean-Pierre de Caussade, *Sacrament of the Present Moment* (San Francisco: Harper & Row, Publishers, 1982), 1.

6. Al Ries and Jack Trout, *Positioning: The Battle for Your Mind* (New York: Warner Books, 1981), 11.

7. William James, *Psychology: Briefer Course* (New York: Henry Holt and Company, 1892), 143.

8. Richard Foster, *Celebration of Discipline* (San Francisco: Harper & Row, Publishers, 1978), 33.

9. Dan Landis, Harry Triandis, and John Adamopoulos, "Habit and Behavioral Intentions as Predictors of Social Behavior," *Journal of Social Psychology* 106 (1978): 227-237.

10. William Law, *A Serious Call to a Devout and Holy Life* (Grand Rapids, Michigan: William B. Eerdmans Publishing Company, 1966), 298.

11. Quoted in Louis Gifford Parkhurst, "Charles Grandison Finney Preached for a Verdict," *Fundamentalist Journal* (June 1984): 41.

CHAPTER 3

Gregory the Great, "Commentary on the Book of Job." Quoted in an excellent overall introduction to the topology of prayer study, James Hasting's classic survey work, *The Christian Doctrine of Prayer* (New York: Charles Scribner's Sons, 1915).

William Blake quoted from C. S. Lewis, *Letters to Malcolm: Chiefly on Prayer* (New York: Harcourt, Brace, and World, 1963), 55.

1. See excellent discussions of Aristotle and Plato positions on the development of virtues in Amelie Rorty, "Plato and Aristotle on Belief, Habit, and Akrasia," *American Philosophical Quarterley* 7, 1 (January 1970): 50-61; Cynthia Freeland, "Moral Virtues and Human Powers," *Review of Metaphysics* 36 (September 1982): 3-22.

2. See John Climacus in J.P. Migne, ed., *Patrologia Graeca*, lxxxviii, 585-1248.

3. Blaise Pascal, *Pensees* (New York: Penguin Books, 1966) 149ff. See a good analysis of "The Wager" in an article by Robert Holyer, "Pascal on Belief and the Religious Life," *Scottish Journal of Theology* 35 (1982): 431-445.

4. Martin Luther, *Works of Martin Luther* 1 (Grand Rapids, Michigan: Baker Book House, 1980), 228.

5. L. D. Nelson, and Russell Dynes, "The Impact of Devotionalism and Attendance on Ordinary and Emergency Helping Behavior," *Journal for the Scientific Study of Religion* 15,1 (1976): 47-59.

6. John Calvin, *Institutes of the Christian Religion* 2 (Philadelphia: Westminster Press, 1960), 864.

7. Cassian, "Institutes," *Nicene and Post-Nicene Fathers*, 11 (Grand Rapids, Michigan: Eerdmans Publishing Company, 1978), 161-641.

8. Andrew Murray, *With Christ in the School of Prayer* (Grand Rapids, Michigan: Zondervan Publishing Company, 1983), 63.

9. Soren Kierkegaard, *The Journals of Soren Kierkegaard* (New York: Oxford University Press, 1959), 97.

CHAPTER 4

John Calvin, *Institutes of the Christian Religion* 2 (Philadelphia: Westminster Press, 1960), 866.

John Bunyan, *Prayer* (Swengel, Pennsylvania: Reiner Publications, n.d.), 1.

1. See George Foot Moore, *Judaism* 1 (New York: Schocken Books, 1971), 259.

2. Igumen Valamo, *The Art of Prayer* (London: Faber and Faber, 1966), 241.

3. James Mursell, *How to Make and Break Habits* (Philadelphia: Lippincott, 1953). The author says breaking bad habits means one needs to first understand oneself and the meaning of habits. Once those are understood then techniques to implement decisions are available.

4. Augustine, *Confessions* (New York: Macmillian, New York, 1961).

5. Quoted in Karl Barth, *Prayer and Preaching* (Naperville, Illinois: SCM Book Club, 1964).

6. Phillips Brooks, "Going Up to Jerusalem," *Selected Sermons* (New York: Ayer, Salem, Inc., 1949).

7. R. A. Torrey, *How to Pray* (Springdale, Pennsylvania: Whitaker House Publishing Company, 1983), 6.

CHAPTER 5

Francois Rochefoucauld, *Sentences and Moral Maxims* (New York: French and European Publications, 1976) Maxim 70.

Isaac Bashevis Singer, "Prayer," *GEO* (February 1983): 81.

1. A. Ellis, *Reason and Emotion in Psychotherapy* (New York: Lyle Stuart, Inc., 1962).

2. Thomas Aquinas, *My Way of Life* (New York: Confronternity of the Precious Blood, 1952), 35.

3. See also Scott Peck's excellent discussion of modern man's weak attempts to love in *The Road Less Traveled* (New York: Simon and Schuster, 1978), 81-184.

4. Cited in Donald Bloesch, *Essentials of Evangelical Theology* 2 (San Francisco: Harper and Row, 1978), 56.

CHAPTER 6

E. M. Bounds, *Power Through Prayer* (Grand Rapids, Michigan: Baker Book House, 1972), 36.

Arnold Dallimore, *Spurgeon* (Chicago: Moody Press, 1984), 14.

1. Tertullian, "On Prayer," *Ante-Nicene Fathers* 3 (Grand Rapids, Michigan: Eerdmans Publishing Company, 1980), 690.

2. Quoted in *Context*, June 1, 1983, p. 4, from Soren Kierkegaard, *Parabola*.

CHAPTER 7

Cited by Martin Marty in *Context* (October 1984): 2.

Shel Silverstein, *A Light in the Attic* (New York: Harper and Row, 1981), 15.

CHAPTER 8

Jacques Ellul, *Prayer and Modern Man* (New York: The Seabury Press, 1970), 99.

1. Allen O. Miller and M. Eugene Osterhaven, *Heidelberg Catechism* (New York: Pilgrim Press, 1963).

2. Richard John Neuhaus, "Unsecular America," *The Religion and Society Report* 1, 1 (June 1984): 2.

3. C. S. Lewis, *Letters to Malcolm: Chiefly on Prayer* (New York: Harcourt, Brace and World, Inc., 1963), 23.

4. Harry Emerson Fosdick, *The Meaning of Prayer* (New York: The Association Press, 1938), 142.

5. O. Hallesby, *Prayer* (Minneapolis, Minnesota: Augsburg Publishing House, 1975), 44-45.

6. Martin Buber, *Tales of the Hasidim* (New York: Schocken Books, 1961).

CHAPTER 9

C. S. Lewis, *Letters to Malcolm: Chiefly on Prayer* (New York: Harcourt, Brace and World, 1963), 116.

John Chrysostom, "Homilies on Ephesians (Homily xvi)," *Nicene and Post Nicene Fathers XIII* (Grand Rapids, Michigan: Eerdmans Publishing Company, 1979), 127.

1. Knight Dunlap, *Habits* (New York: Liveright Publishing Company, 1947), 186.

2. Frederick Kanfer, "Self-Management Methods," *Helping People Change* (New York: Pergamon Press, 1980), 341.

3. G. R. Liem, "Performance and Satisfaction As Affected by Personal Control over Salient Decisions," *Journal of Personality and Social Psychology* 31 (1975): 232-240.

4. T. A. Brigham and A. Stoerzinger, "An Experimental Analysis of Children's Performance for Self Selected Rewards," *Behavioral Analysis in Education* (Dubuque, Iowa: Kendall-Hunt Publishing, 1976).

5. F. Heider, *The Psychology of Interpersonal Relationships* (New York: John Wiley and Sons, 1958).

6. D. Martyn Lloyd-Jones, *Spiritual Depression: Its Causes and Cure* (Grand Rapids, Michigan: Eerdmans Publishing Company, 1973), 2-21.

7. Stanton Peele, "Out of the Habit Trap," *American Health* (September/October 1983): 42ff.

CHAPTER 10

P. T. Forsyth, *The Soul of Prayer* (Grand Rapids, Michigan: Eerdmans Publishing Company, 1916), 11.

Karl Barth, *Prayer and Preaching* (Naperville, Illinois: SCM Book Club, 1964), 21.

1. Stanton Peele, "Out of the Habit Trap," *American Health* (September/October 1983): 42ff.

2. Igumen Valamo, *The Art of Prayer* (London: Faber and Faber, 1966), 204-205.

3. Forsyth, *Soul*, 11.

4. Donald Bloesch, *The Struggle of Prayer* (San Francisco: Harper and Row Publishers, 1980), 147.

5. Samuel Chadwick, *God Listens* (Westchester, Illinois: Good News Publishers, 1973), 8.

CHAPTER 11

Stanton Peele, "Out of the Habit Trap," *American Health* (September/October 1983), 42ff.

1. Stanton Peele, *Love and Addiction* (New York: Taplinger Publishing Company, 1975), 36.

2. Paul Y. Cho and Harold Hostetler, *Successful Home Cell Groups* (South Plainfield, New Jersey: Bridge Publications, 1981).

3. Paul Billheimer, *Destined for the Throne* (Fort Washington, Pennsylvania: Christian Literature Crusade, 1975).

4. Roy Hession, *My Calvary Road* (Grand Rapids, Michigan: Zondervan Publishing Company, 1978).

5. Leroy Festinger, *A Theory of Cognitive Dissonance* (Evanston, Illinois: Row, Peterson, 1953).

6. David Johnson, "Attitude Modification Methods," *Helping People Change* (New York: Pergamon Press, 1980), 79.

CHAPTER 12

C. A. D. Medina, "Reading Habits: A Sociological Approach," *America Latina* (1976): 70-129.

1. Nancy Streltzer, "Influence of Emotional Role Play on Smoking Habits and Attitudes," *Psychological Reports* (1968): 817-820.

2. Catherine de Hueck Doherty, *Poustinia* (Notre Dame, Indiana: Ave Maria Press, 1975).

3. Lyle Schaller, "Human Ethology: The Most Neglected Factor in Church Planning," *Review of Religious Research* 17, 1 (1975): 2-14.

CHAPTER 13

Research and Forecasts, Inc., *American Values in the 80s: The Impact of Belief* (Hartford, Connecticut: Connecticut Mutual Life Insurance Company, 1981), 216.

1. Sam Gill, "Prayer as Person: The Performative Force in Navajo Prayer Acts," *History of Religions* 17, 2 (1977-78): 143-157.

2. Will Sanborn, "When You're Looking for a Pastor," *Leadership* (Summer 1985).

3. John Henry Newman, "Unreal Words," in Warren Wiersbe, *Listening to the Giants* (Grand Rapids, Michigan: Baker Book House, 1980), 23.

CHAPTER 14

T. J. D'Zurilla and M. R. Goldfried, "Problem Solving and Behaviour Modification," *Journal of Abnormal Psychology* 78 (1971): 197-226.

1. Derek Price, "The Unsung Genius: Of Ceiling Wax and String," *Natural History* (January 1984): 49-56.

2. Jacques Ellul, *Prayer and Modern Man* (New York: The Seabury Press, 1970), 143.

3. C. S. Lewis, *Letters to Malcolm: Chiefly on Prayer* (New York: Harcourt, Brace and World, 1963), 22.

4. Brother Lawrence, *The Practice of the Presence of God* (Springdale, Pennsylvania: Whitaker House, 1982).

5. Ignatius Loyola, *Spiritual Exercises of St. Ignatius* (Garden City, New York: Doubleday, 1970).

6. Frederick Kanfer, "The Maintenance of Behavior by Self-Generated Stimuli and Reinforcement," in Jacobs and Sachs, eds. *The Psychology of Private Events* (New York: Academic Press, 1971).

7. "Benjamin Franklin and the Way to Virtue," *American Quarterly 30* (Summer 1978): 199-223.

8. Martin Luther, *Letters of Spiritual Counsel* (Philadelphia: Westminster Press, 1955), 125.

9. L. Homme, *How to Use Contingency Contracting in the Classroom* (Champaign, Illinois: Research Press Company, 1969).

10. R. A. Torrey, *How to Pray* (Old Tappan, New Jersey: Fleming Revell, 1970).

11. D. J. Kiesler, "Some Myths of Psychotherapy Research and the Search for a Paradigm," *Psychological Bulletin, 65* (1965): 110-136.

12. Richard Wertman, "The Ultimate Head Waiter: How the Brain Controls Diet," *The Technology Review* (July 1984).

CHAPTER 15

Igumen Valamo, *The Art of Prayer* (London: Faber and Faber, 1966), 231.

Samuel Chadwick, *God Listens* (Westchester, Illinois: Good News Publishers, 1973), 26.

1. Fred Smith, *You and Your Network* (Waco, Texas: Word, Inc., 1984), 121.

2. Helmut Thielicke, *Our Heavenly Father* (Grand Rapids, Michigan: Baker Book House, 1960), 132.

3. Evelyn Christenson and Viola Blake, *What Happens When Women Pray* (Wheaton, Illinois: Victor Books, 1975), 132.

4. Warren McFarlan quoted in *Computer Decisions* (May 1983).

5. Julie Fitzpatrick Rafferty, "Watching the Biological Clock," *Harvard Magazine* (March/April 1983): 26-29.

CHAPTER 16

Igumen Valamo, *The Art of Prayer* (London: Faber and Faber, 1966), 201.

1. Jacques Maritain, *Prayer and Intelligence* (London: Sheed and Ward, 1942), 5.

2. R. A. Torrey, *How To Pray* (Springdale, Pennsylvania: Whitaker House, 1983), 84-85.

3. Thomas a Kempis, *The Imitation of Christ* (Nashville, Tennessee: Thomas Nelson, 1981), 67.

4. Terry Muck, "Ten Questions About the Devotional Life," *Leadership* (Winter 1982): 34.

5. Samuel Taylor Coleridge, *Confessions of an Inquiring Spirit* (Stanford, California: Stanford University Press, 1957).

6. Quoted in Henry Kissinger, *Years of Upheaval* (Boston: Little, Brown & Co., 1982).

7. From Michael Oakshott, *Wisdom of Conservatism Vol. I* (Mars Hill, North Carolina: Institute for Western Values, 1971), 93.